How to Write a Book:

A Book for Anyone Who Has Never
Written a Book (But Wants To)

Lauren Bingham

Contents

Download The Audio Version of This Book for Free!

If you love listening to audiobooks on the go or enjoy the narration as you read along, I have great news for you. You can download this book for FREE just by signing up for a FREE 30-day audible trial. Go to https://tinyurl.com/n4ktzhnu to download it for free

5 Writing Exercises

If you're interested in learning to write books, chances are high that you've tried before and gotten stuck. As a result, you may be even less enthusiastic about trying again. If that's the case, check out some personally selected writing exercises from author Lauren Bingham's vault of helpful tricks and tips for getting the cursor moving again... or for the first time. Go to https://subscribepage.io/5-Writing-Exer cisesto download your own copy of Lauren Bingham's Five Favorite Writing Exercises.

Introduction

"... And that's how Uncle Lester became known as 'The Amazing Flying Parcheezi!'" You finish your story with a flourish as the crowd that has slowly gathered around you gasps and giggles admiringly, while a smattering of applause slowly fades.

"That was a great story!" someone says.

"Your stories are always so good," another person intones. "You should write a book!"

You blush a little, embarrassed that your off-handed story about your off-the-wall uncle had garnered this much attention. "Well, maybe someday," you mumble, waving off your newfound celebrity. "Maybe someday."

Sometimes that's where the dream ends. You wander back off to work, continue socializing at a cocktail party, or go back to doing whatever it was before you had to spin one of your amazing yarns. But sometimes it's not that easy. You begin to let your mind wander further and further into the hereto-unexplored territory of becoming a published author. It starts with a little nudge like "If I wrote a book, what would it be about?" Then maybe you creep stealthily into "Who would the main characters be?" Before you know it, you've got three plot points scoped out and have made several mental notes to yourself to research whether situation A is possible, whether product B was

available in 1957, and to call your mother, because you can't remember
Uncle Lester's middle name.

It happens to all of us. Once upon a time, I was encouraged to write
a book. And, well, you see how that turned out. I didn't just wake up,
type out a manuscript, and go on with my life, however. It's been a
very long and weird journey from "You should totally write a book,"
to "Would you sign my book?"

I believe that one of the most beautiful things about humans is the
stories they tell. Storytelling has given us names for the stars in the sky
and informs us of our past. The stories told by our ancestors have built
our world, given us clarity in times of need, and continue to enthrall
us as tales from the deepest reaches of the world circulate in written
form.

At the same time, many have scoffed at me or laughed when I
mention that I'm a writer. At first, that used to offend me, but now I
have a stock answer that I think suits me and the purpose quite well:
"Do you ever read?"

Reading is fundamental. While some parties argue that the future
will be controlled by robots, and learning to read will be as useless as
practicing proper handwriting, the fact remains that reading is still
at the core of the process through which those robots will be built.
Others argue that television and audiobooks will soon make reading
obsolete, but again, you can't have television or audiobooks without someone writing a script. Your automatic self-driving car might
recognize the road signs without your input, but someone needs to
program the car so that it can do the reading for you. Plus, even the
lightest of duties, such as arguing on social media, requires at least a
moderate grasp of written language. Reading isn't going anywhere
anytime soon, and as long as there is reading, writers will have a place
in this world.

Therefore, when people indicate that they find writing to be a worthless pursuit, I have to wonder what they're trying to get out of the experience. If your sole purpose in writing is to enjoy the process of committing the words in your brain and the scenarios of your imagination to paper (and/or the screen of some device in modern times), then your efforts will never be in vain. If, instead, your goal is to write a bestseller, get a movie deal, buy yourself a large house, and become extremely popular for your witty Twitter banter, then the chances are very high that your endeavors will be fruitless. Sure, you may be far more talented than the latest bestselling author, but talent is what gets books written. Politics and marketing are what turn them into bestsellers.

If you want to write a book, then write a book. Write a book because you need to write a book. Write a book because you're sick of telling the same story and you just want to email everyone the file and be done with it. Write a book because you don't want anyone to forget about The Amazing Flying Parcheezi. The passion is what makes the project so enjoyable. And if you make any money out of it, so much the better!

Nearly everyone is compelled at some point in their life to turn a thought into a story, a story into a book, and a book into a series. Whether it's a memoir, capturing an oral tale in written format, or weaving a new universe full of fascinating inhabitants who do interesting things, all of us have stories inside us, just bursting to come out. Writing is what gives us the ability to capture all of these things and draw them out into the open from the deep parts of our brain in which they dwell. How can any of us possibly be unworthy of jotting down our thoughts?

That being said, it's only fair to warn you that writing isn't always easy, and it isn't always fun. There are times when you've stared at a blank page without progress for so long, that you start to wonder if you're still literate. You'll stay up all night and get up before the sun rises because you have to "work out this part here." Your writing will interfere with your life, and your life will dramatically cramp your writing style. But if you want to write, then go do it!

This is not a book about how to write a bestseller. This is not about my journey to the top of the *New York Times* list, because I haven't gone there-- nor do I think I'll ever make that particular trek. The quality of the book you write is entirely up to you. I make no promises, as the saying goes, but I'll tell no lies.

Instead, this book is going to be about the writing process. This tool is intended for anyone who is stuck on the teeter-totter of "should I/shouldn't I" when it comes to writing a book. Instead of talking about things like grammar and kerning, we'll be exploring the work that needs to be completed before you even name your manuscript file. We'll skip the helpful tips for writing a marketable plot, but we'll look at staying organized and focused while your tale comes to life. Rather than going through the steps of finding an agent and shopping for a publisher, we'll comfort and calm those going through the editing process for the first time. Fiction or nonfiction, prose or poetry, there's a little bit of something for everyone when it comes to keeping brains happy and spirits high when attempting to crank out your very first literary attempt.

Whether or not this book convinces you to write your own, you will put it down with a confident understanding of what it takes, emotionally, physically, and intellectually, to write your very first book. While I believe that everyone has a story to tell and a platform on which to tell it, only you can decide whether you have the internal fortitude to get through the process.

There's no judgment, either. If this book teaches you that you are not in a place to write a book this very second, then it's done its job. But, if you find yourself taking notes, brainstorming in a secret notebook, or daydreaming your way through significant moments that would be in your book, then maybe it's time to dip a toe or two into the world of writing.

Honestly, the worst thing that could possibly happen is that you never write a book, and that's pretty much how things stand today, isn't it? Regardless of whether this book is a step towards your new super-stardom as a bestselling author or a precious reminder of why you stick to blogging when you need to exercise your writing chops, you're taking a very big step by getting off of that teeter-totter and finding out what it would take to get the job done.

Why Write a Book?

Answering a question with another question is known as "maieutics." In this day and age, it's considered rude, though in Socratic philosophy, it's a necessity. After all, how can we reveal a question's true nature until we have questioned the very question itself? But when you ask yourself why you should write a book, the answer truly is another question: "Why not?"

For many, the process is strange and scary. In fact, even for those of us who have done it a few times, the process remains strange and scary. What if you run out of words? What if you run out of things to talk about? How much time does it take? Am I going to become a recluse? All of those are valid questions, even the "recluse" question. Writing a book can be a very lengthy and passionate undertaking.

There are three main qualities required of those who endeavor to write a book:

1. Time

2. Energy

3. A good sense of humor

Many experts on the topic will say that you need to have a solid plot with intrigue, relatable characters, and a unique writing style to create worthwhile fiction, while nonfiction writers are only deemed good at their art if they write academically and stick to solid facts.

My counter-argument is that while those are very good points, even the most inspirational characters will fail to change lives with their story, and the most accurate factual book in the world will never inform a soul if the author lacks the time and energy to get through the writing process, and the good humor to deal with editing. The worst book in the world is the one no one has written, in my opinion.

So how much time does a book take to write? There's really no set answer to that question. One aspiring author may tackle a topic in segments, researching as they go, and taking their time to flesh out each skeletal section deliberately. On the other hand, some writers have been sitting on a delicious perspective for so long that they can easily type it out in a matter of days, pausing only for meals, bathroom breaks, and double-checking their facts.

Of course, you may have gotten yourself into a situation in which you need to write a book in time to meet a specific deadline. This can be both a blessing and a curse, as you will be forced to trudge along to submit the required assignment, but stressed about keeping yourself on track and able to focus on the topic at hand. There is a certain amount of finesse that is required to set and meet deadlines, and we'll take a look at what it takes to remain cool, calm, and collected in the face of the clock in another section.

If you are writing a book because you want to write a book, and not because anyone is expecting you to do so, then you can plan on it taking as long as it takes. But perhaps, at least for your first effort, you should give yourself a few milestones to complete to keep the process marching along. That could mean deciding where you want to begin and end your book, creating a hypothesis that must be proven, or simply choosing a page number and the date you hope to have that many pages written.

Most writers can bang out a few thousand words per writing session, but they also do a lot of work before, during, and after the writing process itself. The amount of research that can go into a book is absolutely staggering. You might think that fiction lends itself to a little less factual integrity, but you'll still find it's important to find out if your characters can reasonably be behind the wheel of that specific vehicle, based on their time period and income level, or trying to find the right descriptive words for the architecture of the setting you're trying to portray. After all, there's a distinct difference in feel between "Generations of ivy grew unchecked on the facade of the old bungalow, which seemed to crumble before our very eyes" and "Generations of ivy grew unchecked on the glass walls of the skyscraper, giving it a surprisingly cozy ambiance."

Therefore, when you consider the amount of time you're willing to spend on a book, bear in mind that not every moment is going to result in a productive keystroke. You'll backspace, delete, undo, copy, paste, stare into the abyss wonder what you've done, and go back to the drawing board several times. We'll talk about this process in more detail later, as well. But for now, the answer to the eternal question "How long does it take to write a book?" can either be answered with "a month" or "your entire lifetime."

To manage all of this time, you must have energy, as well. Sitting in a chair, typing for hours at a time, can cause all sorts of pain: neck and back pain from remaining seated for so long, wrist anguish from the unnatural position we assume to type, and infinite headaches from staring at a screen for so long. But none of these physical ailments compare to the mental strain of attempting to write a book.

According to many writers-- and actively reinforced by professors, teachers, and many websites on the matter-- you should be able to log 2,000 words a day to be considered an "effective" or "productive" writer. National Novel Writing Month, or NaNoWriMo as it's affectionately known, also encourages writers to exercise their minds and spirit by coughing up at least 2,000 words each day. Truly, this is an admirable number to aspire to, and setting goals is extremely important, as we'll discuss shortly. But there will be days where, as a human with other things to do in your life besides anguish and toil over a simple tome, you might as well wring blood from a stone and find 2,000 entire words that aren't just assorted syllables-- the literary equivalent of noise.

Some may call this affliction "writer's block." I call it what it really is: Running out of energy. Mental, physical, emotional, spiritual... Any deficit in these categories will lead to the brain and hands stubbornly refusing to produce words on a page. And to add insult to injury, you can't just force your way through it, like a profusely bleeding soldier marching stolidly onward through the blasts of fuselage and relentless terror. There are things you can do to redirect what energy you have and possibly conjure up a little inspiration. Every professional writer has their own arsenal of tricks to fool the brain into believing any time is a good time to write, but this is your first book. This isn't your life's devotion (yet). You aren't getting paid (yet). You're just a regular person, writing a single book (so you think) which you'll never do again (so you say). You don't need to know all the professional tips and tricks if you're not going to be a professional, but they can offer you some assistance when you inevitably run out of energy. Should you decide you do need those tips and tricks, you'll find them in the "Helpful Information" section at the end of this book.

As for the last prescription, "a good sense of humor," it should seem pretty logical that the act of writing a book is intensely illogical. Whether you're using a typewriter, a laptop, a quill, or a ballpoint pen, there's nothing simple or straightforward about writing a book. It is simply a necessary activity to which many of us are drawn.

If you don't meet that 2,000-word quota, you need to have the good cheer to simply move on and recognize that Scarlett O'Hara (via Margaret Mitchell) had it right, and "tomorrow is another day." One day might be a 6,000-word day. The next day might yield a mere 6 words. If you overwhelm yourself with the seriousness of being "behind schedule," you'll find yourself creating stress. Stress is best known for its ability to sap all of your available energy. No energy, as we've established, means no book. Don't allow yourself to become stressed.

That's not to say it's important to remain cheerful and delightful every step of the way. The archetype of the artist or creator states that we must be moody and choleric and woeful and always in the throes of romantically piteous agony. My personal suggestion is that you behave as you would normally behave. Just allow yourself a mote of forgiveness if things aren't coming out the way you like.

In fact, for your first effort, I recommend not holding yourself to any sort of expectations. Set milestones, but don't actually carve them in stone. Instead of 2,000 words a day, consider "I'll have gotten through Uncle Lester's childhood years by the end of the month." This way, you have a goal in mind to keep you marching, but it isn't measured by letters or words or hours spent scratching away at your masterpiece. Instead, you can keep track of your progress by your involvement in developing the tale you intend to tell. Making milestones manageable is just one way to keep a sense of humor while you're writing your first opus.

I also strongly recommend that you hold back any urge to edit as you write. Of course, you can backspace or scratch out any misspellings, and if you look at the phrase you've just written and immediately think of a better way to write it, then, by all means, do so. But if you spend every day agonizing over the past 2,000 words, you'll never find the next 2,000 words. Some writers call these "sprints," in which they create a finish line for the day, and simply write, write, write until they reach the finish line. Don't look back; just keep putting one word after another. There will be plenty of time to edit once you've got a full book. In fact, a sentence that looks like utter garbage today might become absolute poetry once you've filled in the paragraphs following it. Provide yourself with enough grace to not micromanage yourself until you've completed the task at hand.

And lastly, on the "sense of humor" topic, I want to urge you to remember that once you have birthed your opus into the world, it will no longer belong to you. It's your original material, of course, and all of the thoughts contained are your own, any likeness or resemblance is purely coincidental and all that, but, it is no longer just your baby. Your baby is going to be read by anyone who gets their hands on it, and it's not going to mean to them what it means to you.

That is to say, once the thoughts are out of your head and on paper (or screen, depending on the format), those who consume those thoughts are going to interpret them in their own way. Someone with different thoughts, opinions, experiences, and understandings is going to look at your work and critique based on what they know.

With any luck, your published book will attract the right kind of reader. This is where intelligent marketing comes in, which we'll certainly touch on later in this book. But inevitably, your book will wander into the hands of someone who just doesn't get it. This person will read what they can, and immediately take to the internet to let everyone know that they found your book to be a wad of mindless drivel that is best used to prop up wonky furniture. Not everyone will love you or appreciate your efforts. It's not personal: it's just an internet review.

One of my first books earned a review that said something to the effect of "everything in this book can be found on the internet." It was a "how-to" book. My first reaction was shock and horror. I thought I'd completely failed. Then I really thought about it. The person who wrote that comment wasn't wrong-- everything in the book really could be found on the internet. But when you think about it, that's exactly how the internet works. If you're doing it right, you should be able to verify every factoid in a "how-to" book via the Internet. I'd be more concerned if you couldn't double-check the author's work in a nonfiction scenario, because if the author made it all up, then it's fiction, right?

Regardless of semantics and critics, allow yourself to brush off the harsh comments. Allow yourself to have patience and kindness with yourself throughout the process, from the pre-work to the reviews and beyond. Acknowledge that this is not going to be easy, but accept reassurance from those who have been there before that it is fully rewarding. Be prepared to ride a Tilt-A-Whirl of emotions, and learn when to provide yourself with a little grace.

If you don't, I assure you that you will learn all of these things throughout the process of creating your first book. But it's a lot easier if you get yourself into a good headspace before you even commit the first word to the file.

Before You Start Writing

Before you start writing a book, you should know what type of book you want to write. In many cases, that's much easier said than done. Some books lend themselves fantastically to a particular genre or format; for example, "How to Write a Book," is obviously going to be a nonfiction book. I could make the whole thing up, but it's much easier to tell the truth than to reinvent the entire process. Besides, who on Earth would make up a mess like this? But for many authors, you have to decide what to do with your concept before you can go much further.

I encourage aspiring writers to do as much daydreaming at this stage as possible. Obviously, you'll want to tone it down when you're doing treacherous things that require the utmost concentration, such as driving a forklift through a crowded warehouse or guiding a Conestoga wagon over rocky mountain passes. But there are plenty of times when we can put down the phone, tablet, Smart Watch, or whatever you use to occupy your mind when it's not in use and do a little constructive daydreaming. This is how you figure out what your book is really about.

When we think about writing a book, we tend to get all tense and serious about it. Instead, approach thinking about a book the same way you think about what you're getting for lunch when you're driving into the office at 7:30 a.m. Dream about it. Make wishlists. Explore different avenues. Think about the words you want to use. Throw around some concepts you'd like to introduce and how they work together. Words are like Tinker Toys, Legos, Lincoln Logs, or whatever building toy you like to use in analogies-- they fit together in many different ways, so play with them to figure out how you want to use them. Keep your efforts loose and natural so they don't sound forced, stressed, or anxious when you finally write them all down.

If you're the type who likes chaos, then you'll keep all of this pre-work in your head. If you like to proceed about life in a nice and orderly sort of way, then you might want to have a journal or jot-pad for this. I personally find notes stressful. If I can't live up to my notes, then I feel like I've failed. Therefore, the only written evidence you'll find of my pre-work is my research and my proposed Table of Contents (TOC). In fact, my proposed TOCs rarely look like my final product, so I'm not even sure they can be forensically linked to each other.

It may take you a few days or daydreams to figure out the simple question of "what is my book going to be," as odd as that may seem. In fact, you might consider this your first challenge as an author: to free yourself from your own expectations and write a book that genuinely reflects the message you want to relay to the public.

If you want to write the story of The Amazing Flying Parcheezi, Uncle Lester, then what's the best way to do it? Should you go for a facts-only family memoir style with interviews from the legend himself? Should you write it in the format of third-person short stories, with a little artistic license taken to give the tales a vivid, life-like quality? You could go dark and mysterious, employing the second-person perspective to engage and immerse the reader in the experience. You can include local colloquialisms to drive home the cozy, family setting. You can paint a full picture with lavish descriptions, or you can allow the reader to play with your characters in their own setting by leaving all of the details to the imagination with minimal wordplay. There are so many choices, and they all belong to you.

In the next chapters, we'll look at how to get organized before writing. The first chapter is for those who are ready to walk on the wild side of fiction, while the second chapter is for those who want to stick with the weird things we already know about in a nonfiction format. Allow me to ruin your misconceptions by informing you that neither is easier than the other, and all writers are deeply challenged by the books they choose to write. Regardless, here are some solid points of advice to help you get organized before you get started writing.

Chapter One

For Aspiring Fiction Writers

I have nothing but admiration for fiction writers. I have written my fair share of fiction, and I've enjoyed the process, but I always feel a bit self-conscious when I'm done. I end up questioning myself and dragging myself through a rabbit hole of "what ifs." "What if Character A had made a different decision in Chapter 4?" "Does Character B's dialogue make them sound like a giant jerk during the big scene in Chapter 10?" "Do we even need Character C?" "Why did I concentrate so much on describing this thing when I hardly even mentioned that other thing?" Fiction is not for the faint of heart or those who have difficulty making decisions. At least, not without a sympathetic editor.

Fiction writing is storytelling without limits. Your story can take place anywhere, at any time, with a cast of any characters you can imagine. Want to drop off one of today's billionaire playboys in feudal Europe of the 1500s? Do it. Need your characters to head out to space for an important plot point? Have them build a rocket out of car parts. As long as you write it, your readers will follow along.

This is where the notion of genres comes in. According to Merr iam-Webster.com, a genre is *a category of artistic, musical, or literary composition characterized by a particular style, form, or content.* Science fiction, romance, fantasy, myth, mystery, horror, and historical fiction are just a handful of examples of different genres. Some stories blend a few different aspects of standard genres; Neil Gaiman's *American Gods* is a highly regarded example of genre-bending.

The fascinating thing about all genres, though, is that each one takes the world as we know it and completely reinvents it. Take, for example, the Harry Potter series. While the story takes place in modern-day England, as we know it, the entire Wizarding society, complete with cultural mores, language, and biological traits has been invented by author J.K. Rowling. There's enough reality for us to understand the character traits, emotions, and actions of her characters, but the fantasy world is completely from the author's own mind.

Does that mean you have to invent an entire world just to write a good fiction book? Not necessarily, but you have to conjure up enough of a world so that your tale has a place where it can reasonably occur. Even though your fictional world may not be tangible, as an author, you know exactly where Main Street and First Avenue intersect. You know what everyone drives, and where they eat dinner. They get their groceries from one of three supermarkets, though there is a farmer's market in the summer. The snooty people are from one neighborhood, and the "across the tracks" area is marked by a specific geographical location.

So then, what happens if you aren't using a time or place that you're as familiar with? Well, you start researching and learn what you need to know in order to create a place of your own. But we're getting just a little bit ahead of ourselves here. For now, we'll settle the debate of "what is fiction?" with "a tale that comes entirely from your imagination, generally subscribing to one or more literary genres."

What does it take to write a spectacular work of fiction that everyone will want to read? You'll need that world that we just talked about-- and shall continue to talk about in greater specifics. You'll need to introduce characters that readers will care about. Those characters will need to be involved in some great conflict, which builds throughout the tale before reaching a climactic turning point, at which point there is some form of resolution or denouement in which all of the dangling threads of your tale are brought to a conclusion.

Sounds really simple, doesn't it? Except if you were to write a story that was as simple as that description, it would be a sentence. "Bill, a good-looking fellow in his early 30s, awoke one morning and nearly fell down the stairs; however, he caught his balance by grabbing onto the railing and continued out the door to his unsatisfactory retail job." By definition, that is a full story, but it's probably not going to sell millions of copies, and the movie would be incredibly short.

Therefore, a good fiction story needs to have more purpose to it than that. This is where the work comes in, and where many people abandon the idea of writing a book in the first place. There are an awful lot of little hazy details that need to be figured out before you start writing, otherwise, you end up with a whole lot of stream-of-consciousness drivel... unless that's what you were going for in the first place, with all due respect to William Faulkner.

To begin your work of fiction, you will need a character map and a plot outline. Some seasoned writers recommend starting with the characters, while others recommend starting with the plot. Both, in my opinion, are incredibly important, so I find it difficult to ignore one in favor of the other. However, both will need to be outlined and unless you have the astounding skill of being able to write two different things with each hand, you'll need to handle them one at a time.

The Character Map

The character map can be a literal map, as the name implies, or an Excel spreadsheet, or a very organized list. You can use pictures to help you visualize your characters, or jot down the details of their appearance. The point of a character map is to bring out all of the potential characters in your tale and to establish who they are, how they're connected to each other, and the roles they play within your story. There are plenty of templates of character maps available online, some of which I've linked to at the end of this book; however, you also have the option to free-form list this information in a way that makes sense to you.

That last bit-- "in a way that makes sense to you"-- is really crucial for the prework. Your notes need to be thorough enough so that you can glance at them and know exactly what you meant. This can be somewhat difficult if your characters summon you from a deep sleep, or while you're changing lanes on a major freeway, but be as detailed as it's safe and sane to be when making your notes. There is nothing quite so frustrating as looking at your notes to see something vague like "don't forget Elizabeth's hair," only to realize you have not only forgotten Elizabeth's hair but who Elizabeth is in the first place. Instead, something like "Elizabeth, Penn's sister, is always brushing her hair, which is why Penn is implicated at the crime scene when a long blonde hair is discovered on the body" will better serve you to keep everyone and everything organized.

So who are your characters? Who do you include on your map? Your protagonist, of course, or the hero of your tale. The term "hero" does not mean they have to behave like Superman or Captain America. Instead, this indicates that it is the actions of this person, along with their reactions, that will help develop the plot of this tale. There can be more than one protagonist, although generally speaking, only one steps into the lead role. For example, there are plenty of wizards and witches who keep things moving along in the *Harry Potter* series, but there's also a reason it's not called the *Harry Potter and Friends* series. Young Harry is written into a role that requires some heavy lifting, emotionally speaking, so he is the main protagonist.

Then you've got the antagonist. Traditionally speaking, we think of the antagonist as "the bad guy" or "the villain." This is a bit of a misnomer because the antagonist isn't obligated to be morally evil; instead, this character opposes the protagonist. They help generate and perpetuate the conflict at the center of the story. Romeo and Juliet's parents, for example, aren't inherently evil. They just happen to be participants in a long-standing strife. It's technically the familial feud-- and their participation therein-- that causes the tragic end to the star-crossed lovers' lives. But they are still considered the antagonists of their tale.

Therefore, when you're dreaming up your characters, think less in terms of "good guy/bad guy," and more in terms of "people perpetuating conflicting opinions." It's your choice from there to emphasize the morality or evil of their roles.

Then there are supporting characters. Supporting characters often get a reputation as being afterthoughts or leftovers, but they're actually the main reason the plot moves along in the first place. You could write a novel in which the protagonist and antagonist only interact with each other. However, from the standpoint of the reader, it's often helpful to have additional characters around to keep the story moving forward. In *The Girl Who Loved Tom Gordon*, by Stephen King, a large portion of the story follows a little girl wandering alone in the woods. Yet we know that she has a family waiting for her. Her hopes of being reunited with her family-- the supporting characters-- are what drive the plot forward while she wanders.

Supporting characters do all sorts of wonderful things. They can demonstrate the social norms. They can be sounding boards for the protagonist and antagonist. They can be the voice of reason or the devil's advocate. They can show the readers the truth that the protagonist and antagonist can't see because they're too wrapped up in their own worlds. They can be friends, family, housemates, love interests, or people who have managed to walk into the same shop at the same time as one of the main characters.

So how many characters is the right number of characters? That depends substantially on what you're using them for. A traditional Greek chorus includes up to 50 performers, but there's no particular requirement. As the author, it is your prerogative to give every citizen in town a voice or to simplify your story by limiting the number of speakers with backstories.

There are a few things to keep in mind when it comes to choosing your roster of characters, and the map you create can help you organize these tenets of character building. First, there's a difference between full-blown characters and people who happen to show up in your story. For example, if you have a scene taking place at a grocery store, the elderly lady who asks for assistance in putting a watermelon in her cart, interrupting your protagonist's train of thought, doesn't necessarily have to be a complete character, unless it makes sense to give her a name, a backstory, a full purpose in the plot, a relationship to the protagonist, and a specific role in the overall quest. She can, but that's up to you and how much time you want to spend detailing all of this information to readers if she's never going to appear again.

Next, consider what a potential character will provide to the overall plot. If, for example, you decide to write in the very popular trope of the love triangle, make sure it has something to do with the story. If Matt is trying to decide whether he loves Rebecca or Renee, and the reader never actually meets Renee, then why do we even care about her? What purpose does she have in the story? Unless you very clearly indicate how Matt's resilient passion for the mysterious and unseen force of Renee is impeding his ability to behave appropriately, clouding his judgment, or causing him to do cruel things to Rebecca, for example, then it's really not important for the reader to know very much about Renee.

Furthermore, you don't need to write an entire dossier on each person who steps into the book. That may seem like a direct conflict with the "make the characters count" advice, but it's actually part of the same tip. Try to think of your characters as friends you are introducing to your reader. You aren't going to share every intimate detail you know about them, such as their favorite color is orange, their favorite drink is a gin tonic, and the last time they got a haircut was in February unless all of those details are important to the future relationship between the character and the reader. At the moment that Maya is hanging from the side of a helicopter with a machete, flying towards a burning building, we don't need to know that she was born in a small town in Oklahoma, loves green beans, and once had a pet duck named Pyjamas. It would be helpful, however, to know that she spent four years training with a Russian gymnastics team as part of her undercover role with the CIA, but how you choose to reveal that information to the reader is up to you as the author.

Lastly, it's always a good idea to give each character an entrance, a duty, and an exit, especially if they do something significant within the plot. That doesn't mean we have to follow them around every day through the entire story, but even the elderly woman at the grocery store can wheel her cart up to the protagonist, ask for assistance, and then dutifully disappear in the "Cereal and Breakfast Foods" aisle. Having someone appear, do something very important, leave a lasting impression in the readers' minds, and then just vanish like they never existed can be very distracting and confusing to readers. They can walk away, get in their ca,r and drive off, go home, or get Raptured up during the climax of your story, just as long as it makes sense within the context of the story for them to stop appearing.

As you can see, there's a lot to organize when it comes to creating characters, which is what makes the concept of a character map so very handy. You can see who is who, when they enter and leave the story, what they contribute to the plot, and what we need to know about them to understand their role. Some very talented writers can do all of this without making notes. I am not one of them. Therefore, I always recommend those trying out this whole "writing thing" for the first time at least start with a character map. If you turn out to be an ingenue, then you haven't done anything to hinder the process, and if it just so happens that you need a little help with the organization process, then you're already set up for success!

The Plot Outline

Alongside the character map, you'll need to create a plot outline. A plot outline allows you to map out how you're going to get from Point A, meaning the first page of your story, to Point B, when the first part of the rising action occurs, to Point C, and so on until you've reached the natural conclusion of your tale.

Before your head starts whirling at the idea of having bitten off more than you can chew, let's step back a moment to look at what constitutes a plot:

1. Exposition or introduction

2. Rising action

3. Climax or turning point

4. Falling action

5. Resolution or denouement

The exposition or introduction is just that. This section of your story establishes where we are, who the characters are, and in a sense, why we care. One of my favorite examples of a very neat and tidy exposition is the Prologue to William Shakespeare's *Romeo and Juliet*:

Two households, both alike in dignity,
In fair Verona, where we lay our scene,
From ancient grudge breaks to new mutiny,
Where civil blood makes civil hands unclean.
From forth the fatal loins of these two foes
A pair of star-crossed lovers take their life;
Whose misadventured piteous overthrows
Do with their death bury their parents' strife.
The fearful passage of their death marked love,
And the continuance of their parent's rage,
Which, but their children's end, naught could remove,
Is now the two hours traffic of our stage;
The which if you with patient ears attend,
What here shall miss, our toil shall strive to mend.

Everything you need to know before the characters take the stage is laid out here. The location is Verona, Italy. We're about to meet two well-to-do families, and their children are going to fall in love. Sadly, it's not going to end well. Shakespeare even does us the favor of letting us know the whole thing should take about two hours to get through.

Your introduction doesn't have to be in iambic pentameter, of course; prose is fine. You also don't have to feel the need to be as quick about it. Depending on the length of your book and the story you're going to tell, you can spend pages upon pages and entire chapters building towards the point of your story, as long as everything you say is important to the journey.

Deciding what's important to the journey is the whole point of the plot outline in the first place. Sure, you can just open a Word document and wing it, but you're going to need to keep track of where all of your characters are at all times, what subplots are unfolding and why, and most of all, you'll need to figure out why your audience cares about all this. Sure, it's fun to write a whole bunch of intimate and outlandish details, but does your intended reader want to read all of it?

Take, for example, Bram Stoker's description of the setting in Chapter 16 of *Dracula*:

"Never did tombs look so ghastly white. Never did cypress, or yew, or juniper so seem the embodiment of funeral gloom. Never did tree or grass wave or rustle so ominously. Never did bough creak so mysteriously, and never did the far-away howling of dogs send such a woeful presage through the night."

While it's true that Stoker used a lot of words here to establish the fact that "it was really creepy outside," he did so for a reason. He's setting the scene with words and phrases that would be meaningful to his intended audience. There was no television or radio at the time.

People of his era had a limited understanding of the world around them, bolstered by occasional travel and getting their hands on books such as *Dracula*. These words would have chilled them to the very bone, while readers today might read these words thinking "Yes, yes, it's creepy- just get on with it!"

Therefore, when creating your introduction to your tale, think of what your readers want or need to know about the world they are preparing to enter and hook them in by writing to them in the same tone that you would tell this story to them if you were speaking out loud. While you should never write a book for anyone but yourself, you should communicate in words that emphasize the message you are delivering.

Once you've made sufficient introduction, it's time to start weaving in the rising action. One common first-time misconception is that the introduction/exposition and the rising action can't happen at the same time. There is no particular formula that states that pages 1-32 should be exclusively expository and the rising action should begin promptly on page 33. Consider how many different types of literature there are, how many genres and styles make up the literary world, and how the very act of telling a story can change shape even as the story unfolds. *Dracula,* for example, is told through letters and diary entries. The Harry Potter series is told in third person narrative. Both of them deal with interweaving the rising action in different ways.

If you recall from earlier, I mentioned that "reading is fundamental," and this is why. To write a book, you must understand books. I'm not suggesting you copy any one author, completely adopt a tone that's entirely unlike your own, or do anything that might skitter into the world of plagiarism. Instead, I'm asking that you read a lot so you can get a feel for how books work. The more you read, the more options you have for understanding how your own book works.

Take, for example, two of the books mentioned so far: The rising action in *Dracula* takes place slowly, in tiny steps, to thoroughly invest and creep out the reader. The rising action in *Harry Potter and the Sorcerer's Stone* takes place all at once when a door bursts open and Hagrid steps in to disrupt everything. The swirling, whirling mayhem that ensues reflects and emphasizes Harry's confusion at this whole new world unfurling before him.

So let's look back at your plot outline so far. You've got notes on what needs to be covered in the exposition, and then what you hope to achieve in the rising action, and you're not entirely sure how you're going to do that. Some writers like to flesh things out as they create their plot outline. Others-- myself included-- like to get the whole skeleton out before they start adding limbs.

That brings us to the climax, or turning point. This is the point of no return. All of the conflict in your tale so far has brought us to this moment: the final battle, the face-off, the big decision, the crowning moment. It is very easy to shirk away from a big climactic scene. In fact, all throughout my scholastic career, I got marks for "not making enough conflict." Your story doesn't have to have a great big bang, but it does need to make the reader feel and understand the difference between "before" aka- the world revealed in the exposition, and "now," or the way things will be after the climax.

Stephen King does glorious battle scenes that really reflect how we deal with our demons, both internal and external. Harry Potter whips out the wand. Romeo and Juliet end their lives in a tomb. Every story has some major event where the main character realizes they can't continue doing things the way they did before, and they make a very important change. Some just do it with magic and poison.

Once you've decided what the climax is going to be, you might suddenly think about all the things that you can include in the rising action to help you get to that point. Write all of those things down, even if they're in conflict with each other and can't possibly make too much sense if all used at once. Your plot outline is about possibilities and potential; you'll make the tough decisions later.

From the climax, you then have to figure out a way back down. Generally speaking, the laws of gravity apply to literature as well as anything else, and the falling action takes far less time than the rising action. Basically, now that you've gone in and shaken everything up by having your protagonist face strife and struggle, you've had the climax, and now it's time to clean everything up.

Long ago, a writing professor told us something very important and logical, which, in our quest for belonging among the literary elite, we had forgotten: The purpose of the falling action isn't to make everything tidy and digestible for the reader. Instead, it is intended to demonstrate how things are different. You spent the introduction painting a portrait of life in the "before times," you spent countless pages building up the drama and tension to demonstrate how change was going to be difficult, and then you've got the climax, in which your protagonist is forced to make some sort of major change. Now the reader needs to know what's different and why.

This falling action leads to a resolution or denouement. This is where you wrap things up for this particular tale. This does not, however, have to be the so-called "end" of things. If you have a sequel or series in mind, you might want to make sure you keep enough metaphorical doors and windows open to allow for the next tale. Another option is the oft-complained-about ambiguous ending, wherein we don't know if everyone went home and had a wonderful day, or if more conflict arose, or if the world in which your characters live simply blinked out of existence. The purpose of the end of the book isn't necessarily to make things all pat and neat, but to provide a finishing point for the story you are telling. While in theory, you could continue writing forever and ever, that's simply not how books currently work.

Ending your book can be very difficult for a variety of reasons. It can be emotional since you've spent hours, days, and months leading up to this point. You might have a hard time figuring out how to get the ending just right so that you've tied up all the loose ends without rushing or over-explaining things. Stay calm. Don't panic. Write what feels like it makes sense. Take a break. Read what you just wrote. Take another break to think it over. Make notes. Revisit and tinker. I personally recommend saving each version of your ending, if you don't use a program that already stores a version history. Don't throw your scribbles into the fire or trash bin until you're absolutely certain you'll never visit them again.

As we wrap up this section on building a plot, I'll share something that is surprisingly not mentioned often in the writing community: All of these things can change. Your first version of your plot outline and the book that you actually wrote may be significantly different. You might start writing according to plan and realize that your antagonist would never do that thing, or your protagonist wouldn't care about a particular situation. It is completely natural to discover new and exciting things about your characters and your story as you're writing it.

More importantly, it's important that you quell any negative reaction you might have to these changes. Let it happen. Write it through. Explore where things are going. If it ends up being totally out of scope or making you unhappy, go back to where you feel things took a wrong turn, and go another direction. Don't stifle your creative flow just because you thought things would go a very specific way. You might just find-- as many before you have-- that you have more than one story you'd like to tell!

And finally, fear not if you have a lot of questions about the actual writing process after reading this-- we'll get further into those specifics shortly.

Making It All "Real"

So now that you've got all the prospective characters semi-fleshed-out, and you've created a basic outline for what you plan on writing, you've got just two chores left:

1. Write a book

2. Make it good

Super simple, right? This is the part where you might feel equal parts prepared and terrified. This is normal. In fact, that feeling is going to be pretty normal from here on out. Regardless, this is when things start to feel "real." And as a prospective author, it's your job to really make it "real."

So how does an author make a completely fake, invented, imagined, and fully contrived world feel "real" to the reader? Research, obtaining resources, and even conducting interviews.

You might be actively objecting as you read these words. "I'm inventing an entire world! I don't need to do research!" I'm terribly sorry to burst your bubble, but everyone needs to do research. Everything you imagine is based, in some part, on what we recognize and understand in this reality. The time it takes your characters to travel from one imagined location to the next city is going to be based on your understanding of distances and the speed of travel as we know it, even if they use a mode of transportation specifically invented by you at this exact moment. From the type of dwelling they live in to the color of their planet, to the distance to the nearest star, you're going to need at least a sliver of reality on which to base your imagination. And you know what makes for good imagination? Thorough research.

That's not to say that everything in your story has to be absolutely accurate. Readers will forgive a cheat here and there if they even notice at all. But when you're describing people, places, situations, animals, and even the food on the table, it helps if you have a clear mental picture of what you're describing. And mental pictures are formed by experiencing a lot of different people, places, situations, animals, and so on. Therefore, taking the time to research these points will help you gain a broader view of the possibilities, which can in turn help you describe them in rich detail. The reward is that the reader will climb on board without question.

The suspension of disbelief is necessary for fiction to work at all. The more detailed your descriptions, the more accurate your tour of your new world, and the more "real" everything feels, even if it's not real at all, the more willing your readers will be to drop any preconceived notions and come along for the ride.

Resources can come in many different packages. If you're trying to truly capture the essence of an experience, whether that's traveling cross-country, climbing a mountain, shooting into space, or whatever you fancy, it's a great idea to hear from those who have actually done those things. Blogs, vlogs, and social media groups for those who have an interest in those activities can really help you gain insight into what people appreciate and detest about those activities. When you write about it like it's real, it becomes real. Therefore, take your time to see what that lifestyle entails.

You may wish to conduct interviews, either via phone, in person, or email/direct message/etc. with those who have expertise regarding the things you're writing about. Right now, that may seem like overkill for a fiction book, but it can be incredibly rewarding to get some different perspectives about a particular activity, lifestyle, scenario, or aspect of your book that you have limited experience or understanding.

In my own experience, I once contacted a gentleman I met through mutual friends regarding his car. I have driven many cars in my life, but I have not driven a 1971 Buick Riviera. This fellow had a 1973 Riviera. We took it for a spin, and I asked him questions about the maintenance, the steering, and the gas mileage, and he even let me push all the buttons. I didn't necessarily use every single detail we discussed, but I felt much more confident about the frequency with which I had my character stop for fuel on his drive, and his radio had the same glitch my new friend's vehicle had. It made for a much more believable scene with confident descriptions, instead of vaguely referencing the automobile and hoping no one would think about it too much.

I could wax on eternally about the benefit of doing substantial research, but to avoid droning on, I'll leave you with this thought: If at any time you find yourself wondering how you could make your book just a little richer, your descriptions a little deeper, and your world just a little more immersive, consider heading to the web or popping open a book to go the extra mile with your research.

At the end of the day, what you actually do before you start writing your novel is up to you. I certainly recommend a character map and a plot outline, and I encourage you to do as much research before you get started as possible, but sometimes that little word, "possible," gets in the way. For some writers, the best way to get started is to just sit down and start typing, fill in the character map along the way, and jot down the plot outline as you start thinking of it, scribbling with one hand while the other attempts to type. I, myself, have once awoken with a story that was burning so brightly, that I had no choice but to pull open the laptop at 2 a.m. and start typing everything I could think of. That being said, once I reached the point where the brain worm stopped and I was on my own, you can bet I had my notebook out, writing out everything I knew about the characters and where they were headed.

In the words of one of my mentors, "I don't care how it gets organized, but get some sense in here!" That is to say, if you need to write a bit before you create your map and outline, then do it. I will say, however, that the earlier you start organizing in the process, the easier it will be to continue to stay organized, especially when it comes to little fiddly things, like small but very important characters, or subtle plot details that carry all of the subtext of your story. Set yourself up for success, not stress.

Chapter Two

Non-Fiction, Please; I'm Trying to Cut Back

Non-fiction, as the name implies, is the absence of fiction. These books are based on facts and are used to share information to discuss, educate, and raise questions for debate amongst your audience. Many people think of nonfiction as dry and boring, but it really doesn't have to be. Consider these various genres:

- History

- Biography

- Philosophy

- Religion and spirituality

- Politics

- Scientific research

- Business

- Self-Help

- Travel

- How-To

These are just a few of the subjects included in the realm of non-fiction. Non-fiction books can be informative or educational expository writing, persuasive pieces that prove a point, contain arguments that attempt to change the readers' minds, descriptive pieces that take readers to an entirely different time or place, or a narrative of a true event, place, or person. Some people feel that nonfiction should not include opinions or use a casual tone, but get a few pages into a Bill Bryson book or guitarist Slash's autobiography, and you'll see that's not always the case.

Non-fiction books can use a variety of different tones to express their content. The tone an author uses is directly dependent on several factors:

- The content

- The audience

- The intention

The content is your book's topic and the angle you choose to explore. A biographical piece in reverence to Pope John Paul II and a biographical account exploring Billy the Kid's role in establishing the economy of the Wild West would have entirely different tones, due to the subject matter at hand. Similarly, a book detailing how to fix the mechanical pieces of a Volkswagen Beetle and a book guiding you through daily meditation practices would read differently, too.

The audience is also important when choosing the tone of your nonfiction piece. Most people prefer to read books that come across as a conversation with a like-minded friend. If your audience is mostly teenagers, you'll use an entirely different tone than you would writing the business advice of a Fortune 500 CEO.

Lastly, the overall intention of your book will dictate the right voice to use when writing it. The intention is somewhat of a secondary piece to the topic, angle, and audience. Essentially, this is the effect you want your book to have on people. Do you want them to finish the book with a bit of admiration for Billy the Kid? Do you want them to have enough information to write a basic essay on your book for their science exam? Or do you want them to feel like they have a blueprint for the next chapter of their own lives? What you aim to do with your words significantly impacts how you use them.

So now that you have carved out a bit of headspace for your nonfiction book, it's time to do the prework.

Choose a Topic

Choosing the topic of your nonfiction book is possibly the easiest part of the process. Chances are very good that you've had something on your mind lately. Perhaps you've been casually obsessing over a period in history, or you've always been interested in a specific individual who has walked this planet. We all have that "something" that we know a bit more about than the average person.

On the other hand, you may wish to write about something simply because it is unfamiliar, and you want to share your exploration of this new topic with the world, allowing them an intimate look at your learning and growing processes. This is not unheard of, especially in travel books. The journal format is very popular, as it gives others insight into the process and encourages others to do the same.

Your topic may be very broad at first. You might decide to write about pyramids, for example, but that's a vast subject. Which culture? Which continent? Which type of pyramids? You see where this is headed. You can endeavor to write a book that discusses every pyramid known to date, but you're going to need to consider how you plan to do that. A picture and a short blurb of each one? A region-by-region guide with a map and brief history? The possibilities are overwhelming.

Therefore, I recommend you allow yourself some time to really sit and cogitate on your topic. Perhaps you write down the topic you have in mind, in the shortest form possible. Then you give it some thought. Run to the library or do a Google search of that topic, using the same term you did when you wrote it down. Let yourself go down the proverbial rabbit hole. Figure out what you love about it. Learn new things about your topic. Not only will this help you narrow down the points you want to make regarding your subject, but it will also inspire greater confidence that you're heading in the right direction.

Perhaps, however, you're starting with a topic that's already pretty niche. You are certainly permitted to take the rabbit hole journey as well; you might discover new facts that you wish to highlight in your book that bolster the discussion you have in mind. Regardless, write down your very well-specified topic, and start brainstorming.

From the main topic, you'll want to come up with some of the main points you want to make with your book. If it's a biography, what are the main points of your subject's life that you wish to cover? If it's a self-help book, what are the steps that someone must complete to reach the intended outcome? If you're writing a history of a location, what is the timeframe or period you'd like to highlight? While it would be wonderful if someone would write a book about absolutely everything of all time, that's a bit impractical, especially for your first outing.

Take your time with this. I speak from experience when I say there's nothing as frustrating as starting a nonfiction book and realizing about six pages in that there's really no book there. You may find that you can write a compelling essay, but certainly not an entire book. Or perhaps there simply aren't enough resources to allow you to fully investigate the topic. Experts may have just as many questions about it as you do. Go down as many rabbit holes as you need to. Talk to your friends. Get in arguments about it on social media. Whatever it takes to help you really get your topic into focus with enough material to write a complete book on the matter.

My personal favorite format is the outline. Some people prefer maps, swimlanes, or lists, but I love a good outline. I start by typing out the main topic. Then I let the main ideas come out. Under each main idea, I then include the points I would like to make about that idea. From the points, I add my evidence, opinions, or supporting facts. The process takes me about a week because I keep changing it. Sometimes I'll submit an outline to a publisher with notes describing what I think might change. Sometimes I'm completely wrong. The point is that your first outline is rarely more than a good starting point to help you get your thoughts in order.

One thing your outline will reveal is where you'll need more information. You might find yourself winding into a really great discussion area, but in doing so, discover that this is an area where you might need to return to the rabbit hole. Some authors will say that this means you've found a dead end, and you need to go back to the start of the maze. I say this is a great opportunity to reveal your discovery to the readers with the same awe it's giving you at this moment. The fact that you are learning something about which you are passionate may indicate that other individuals have never considered this particular view or aspect of the same topic. You can avoid the unknown, or write it into your discussion because it is unknown.

Once you've got an outline that you're satisfied with, or at least one that doesn't give you massive anxiety, you'll be able to see more clearly what thoughts you have about your topic. From here, you can decide what angle you'll take to discuss your topic.

Explore Your Angle

Another common misconception regarding works of nonfiction is that they do not contain any opinions or bias. This is not true across the board. A travel journal, for example, has no choice but to be written from the point of view of the person traveling. It's impossible to be unbiased when you're writing about your own experiences from your own perspective.

In other cases, however, it's a good idea to remain as unprejudiced as possible with a catalogue-like approach, but that's entirely dependent upon the angle you wish to take.

The "angle" is how you will go about investigating your topic. For example, in this book, I've chosen to go with a very candid, casual approach to the topic of "how to write a book." I chose this angle because I think there are enough formal books on the topic, and I imagine there are quite a few people who need a friendly voice who knows what they're talking about to push them into doing the deed once and for all.

When it comes to your book, will you approach it as a passionate argument? A desperate plea? A scientific study? A historical collage?

A gentle coaxing? One example I like to use when explaining different angles is that of the self-help book. Some of us need to be yelled at to get our lives straight. Others of us need to be subconsciously guided by the subtext that allows us to make our own decisions. What style are you going to use to approach your topic?

The angle will also become evident from the outline you have created. You may have originally thought that you were going to do a completely unbiased history of birth control methods, only to realize somewhere in the creation of the outline that you simply cannot avoid including your own emotions and opinions on the topic. That doesn't mean you've chosen a bum topic; it simply means you will need to adjust your angle.

One way to approach your angle is to ask yourself "What do I want my audience to take away from this book?" In the example mentioned earlier, "a biographical account exploring Billy the Kid's role in establishing the economy of the Wild West," do you want them to have a higher opinion of Billy the Kid or a less favorable impression of early American economic values? You can guide the audience to understand the topic in a certain light. You can't necessarily make them agree with you, or change their own appreciation of the topic, but you do want them to feel they understand your own insight regarding the topic. The angle you choose takes the reader on a very specific voyage, so make sure they know exactly what to pack to take the trip alongside you.

Organize Again

At this point, you've chosen your topic. You've constructed your outline. You've examined your outline to get a feel for your angle.

Now it's time to revisit everything you've done so far and get it fully organized to create the map of where you're heading.

From your outline, you should be able to create a working table of contents for your book. Your table of contents may not follow the same flow as your final outline, because your angle may have changed how your discussion occurs. Additionally, you may look at your outline and discover it doesn't actually fit the schematics of basic chapters, after all.

Much as your first outline isn't necessarily your final outline, your first table of contents doesn't have to be your last. I simply suggest that you turn your outline into a rudimentary draft of your table of contents to help you discover the order in which you'll be writing your book. In non-fiction, point tends to lead to point, and facts support arguments, which means you might find yourself backtracking on yourself if you were to write things in a specific order. Make sure your discussion or argument is presented in an order that makes sense based on your angle. Take your Uncle Lester, for example. The topic of the story is how he became "The Amazing Parcheezi." Perhaps you take the angle that he was absolutely destined to earn this moniker based on events that happened throughout his life. Presenting your details chronologically starting with his birth and continuing through how he lived up to the nickname following its bestowal would make sense, in this regard.

Of course, there are a great many topics that don't lend themselves to any type of chronology. That's why taking the time to reorganize yourself will help you create a cohesive journey through your topic and lend further merit to your angle. I've included a few techniques to help guide you through some possibilities for your own nonfiction work in the Resources section, but for now, consider the overall "case" you're presenting. What is your thesis, or point you're trying to prove (if any)? That should be stated in your Introduction, or at the very beginning of the book. Then think of the facts that lead towards that particular conclusion. Which is the strongest? Which is going to take the greatest amount of time to discuss? Can you create an equally long chapter for each fact, or are some of them technically sub-facts that could nestle closely with a larger, more pressing piece of information?

Putting together a nonfiction book is somewhat like putting together a jigsaw puzzle; however, while a puzzle has a definite singular correct solution, your book does not. The final format that you settle upon is beneficial to you, as it will make the flow of your writing feel much more familiar and be gentle on your brain as you compile your massive piles of facts. At the same time, the organization of your book should make sense for your reader, as well. Your reader doesn't want to be confused, overwhelmed, underwhelmed, or feel like they're losing their mind. For example, if you're bringing up a particular example several times throughout a book, either consider a different arrangement or acknowledge this for your reader. I recall a particular example from earlier in my career, wherein certain aspects of a specific city were mentioned six times throughout the book. On the second mention, I thought perhaps I needed a nap. On the third use, I thought I might be going a little mad. By the fourth time, this information popped up, I actively started flipping through the book to make sure I wasn't losing my mind. Sometimes this is unavoidable, but make sure you alert the reader. And try not to use the same sentences over again. Readers hate that.

You may be thinking that this is a lot of favors for your reader, and that's somewhat true. But what is the purpose of a book if not for the reader? We've discussed the concept of "audience" a few times so far, so you have considered for whom you're writing the book and what purpose you want it to serve. But now I'm telling you that you have to reorganize your entire outline just so the readers will like it.

If you never intend anyone to read your book, then really, you don't need to follow any of this advice-- just go for it! Stop reading this at once and go make your dreams come true!

For the rest of us, however, who at least want our book to go over well at the family holiday party, creating a flow of details throughout your piece is crucial to gaining the appreciation of the reader. Have you ever started reading a book, only to stop halfway through because it wasn't capturing your attention? That experience is exactly why you need to at least somewhat include the reader in the experience of writing a book.

Ultimately, the act of writing is a bit of a compromise between the author and the reader. You're going to write the book you want to write, with the understanding that the resulting product should be something the reader wants to read. And believe it or not, that's usually easier than you might imagine.

Research, Resources, and Interviews

A work of nonfiction will require substantial research. There are always facts to validate, points to prove, and references to include in your work to support your writing.

Even in the case of a personal work, such as a memoir or travelogue, you'll help substantiate your information with factual details. For example, rather than vaguely mentioning that Uncle Lester was born in a summer month at the turn of the century, you'll gain more credibility by saying he celebrates each 29 July. In the travelogue example, you'll greatly aid your reader and yourself by being able to mention where you are, where you're going, and how you're getting there.

There are unknown details about everything, even if you consider yourself a walking encyclopedia on a particular topic. At the end of this book, you'll find a Resources section. I would love to say that those are links that I exclusively hand-picked for my dear readers so they can grow and blossom as writers, but for the most part, they're the materials I used myself to organize my thoughts and make sure I wasn't telling you a bunch of bologna. I truly want you to grow and blossom, which is why I made it a point to share with you only information that I would use.

Since this is rarely a situation where "any old resource will do," it's a fantastic idea to really take your time in the research stage. I personally recommend looking up even the facts that you feel you know for certain, for the mere fact of corroborating your data with multiple resources. For example, I recently wrote a piece about a subject I know so well, that I've been certified in it several times. In theory, I could have simply sat down and written a stream-of-consciousness brain dump of everything I know, and it would have been true. But it wouldn't have been good, and I wouldn't have had the facts on board.

Another great thing research can do is remind you of other things that go hand-in-hand with your main points. Sometimes, as writers, our focus is so strictly placed on a particular piece of information that we block out knowledge that goes hand-in-hand with those facts. It's very much a "forest-and-trees" situation, wherein you're drilling down to a certain point so enthusiastically that you forget to mention all of the supporting details that are really important to the cause. Once upon a time, I was called upon to host a dinner for some prospective clients. They were chefs, so I wanted to serve some simple but flavorful foods to demonstrate that I had been paying attention and doing my research on the topic they were pitching to me that evening. I found some very reputable resources, and I followed the recipes to the absolute letter. Nearly everything turned out beautifully, except for one particular dish. It looked nothing like the photos. Instead of looking like a fluffy beige spread, it was a wet, lumpy brown mess.

When my guests arrived, I had no choice but to serve it. I explained the situation and tried to laugh it off. They asked if I had done this and that while making it. I had not. "This" and "that" were not mentioned anywhere in the recipe I had followed. We took a look at my resource together and discovered that in the author's zest for explaining the history and cultural importance of the dish, they forgot to mention that the reader was supposed to peel a certain ingredient at a very specific time in the process.

The moral of this story is twofold:

1. Do not lose focus of a really important fact

2. Double-check your resources

It is far too easy to stop researching when you find the information you want. If something seems a bit untoward, it usually is. If I had looked for another recipe, I would have very quickly discovered the missing data. Instead, I looked at what I had and said, "Good enough!" While my prospective clients found the whole thing hilarious and hired me anyway, consider how your book will be received by people who don't know you directly and aren't able to hear your apologies and justifications for the error. Write it right the first time and earn the reader's trust for a lifetime.

On the topic of author accountability, resources can always be a bit of a mixed bag. In addition to spreading vast information, we're more aware than ever that the internet can also make misinformation viral in mere moments. This is another reason I like to recommend fact-checking nearly everything. From updates within the scientific community that invalidate previous theories to updates in details surrounding your topic, it's never a bad idea to see what the community at large believes to be the "truth." Some inaccuracies may be unavoidable-- imagine writing an article about the Golden State Killer being at large on 23, April 2018, just one day before police announced they had arrested Joseph DeAngelo for the crimes. I had the pleasure of writing a long piece about a particular celebrity's emotional quest for motherhood that was published the very same day she announced her pregnancy. The saving grace for my career and that of the publisher of that particular outlet was that the rest of my article was a well-researched compilation of her own words on the matter. I was accused of knowing the future, but that's entirely not true!

Another type of resource that can be both a blessing and a curse is the interview. If you can get a first-hand account of anything related to your topic, it will lend credibility and integrity to your piece. Except for one small problem: Interviewees aren't always accurate. That's not to say that they're all filthy liars, but that we are all but human. We remember things incorrectly. Details can get blurry over time and multiple retellings. We may start to confuse situations and transpose a few ingredients within our memories. And yes, some people are filthy liars.

Additionally, there's an interesting phenomenon in which experts might not agree. I encourage anyone who is conducting interviews to get as much perspective as possible on the topic you'll be discussing before actually starting the interview. If they can't get five out of five members of the American Dental Association to agree on the efficacy of a toothbrush, there's not the tiniest chance you'll find two identical versions of the same event.

If you choose to incorporate interviews in your research process, it's a great idea to get contact information so you can follow up with your subject. You may feel you've had an incredibly thorough discussion, yet as you write, you realize you didn't really catch the tone of a particular answer, or the subtext of a response isn't completely clear. If you have the opportunity to clarify that quote or notion, you'll avoid misrepresenting the truth.

So how do you conduct an interview? First, research. Understand what you're going to be talking to this expert about. The most comfortable, informational, and overall successful interviews are more like conversations than a question-and-answer session. You don't have to reach a level of expertise on the topic, but at least know enough that you can participate in a discussion and ask clarifying questions that make sense. There's the famous example of the interviewer who was unaware that Paul McCartney had been in a band before Wings. Just a little bit of research can avoid awkward scenarios such as those.

Next, make sure you're interviewing your subject in a manner that is comfortable for both of you. I learned early in my career that I am incredibly awkward on the telephone. I'd rather take a red-eye flight to Buxtehude for an in-person interview than participate in a lengthy telephone interview. However, if I send my subject some questions via email, I'm more than happy to have a follow-up discussion via telephone. It's strange; I know.

The process of talking to an expert can be somewhat terrifying. Think of it as a conversation. Prepare a list of questions to get you started, but also jot down a list of points you would like to cover throughout the interview. Don't ignore the humanity of your subject. Phrases like "you must have been surprised when you discovered…" or "what was going through your mind when…" or "what was it like to experience…" can give you loads of insight into the interviewee's relationship with the subject at hand, and put a very relatable spin on even the most far-out topics. I once had to interview an investigator who had solved a serial murder and arrested the killer.

I asked exactly one question. The rest of the time, we talked about his role in the crime itself, his headspace since the trial, and his relationship with fellow investigators. At the end of our hour-long chat, he asked if he could contact me again in the future when he was ready to write his autobiography. A good interview can be an amazing experience for everyone involved.

When you're using interviews in your nonfiction work, remember that nonfiction is supposed to reflect reality. The absence of fiction is truth. There are plenty of situations in which parts of interviews are specifically edited, decontextualized, and misconstrued to fit the author's angle. I certainly understand why some writers would choose to do this. To an extent, we all wiggle the truth a bit to get the desired results, both in life and in writing. However, depending on the platform you're using to distribute this not-entirely-true information, there may be consequences. While defamation-- specifically libel-- is treated differently around the world, at the bare minimum it will be a dark mark on your writing career.

Writers have argued since the dawn of the written word whether fiction or nonfiction is "harder" than the other. Having written both myself, I have my own feelings on this matter, but for now, this is going to be one of those debates that may never end. Every author has a comfort zone, which means certain pieces will be much "easier" to write than others. Whether "easier" translates into faster to write, less stressful, minimum research or bountiful source material and imagination remains in the eyes of the beholder, but some books are indeed pleasure cruises while others are as enjoyable as the tour of the S.S. Minnow. That's not to say that all books are a boat wreck, but that some boats are a struggle from the first word and may turn out very different than intended.

Therefore, reflect back to that "sense of humor" I mentioned as a requirement for writing a book. While I've equipped you with various strategies and tools to help guide you through the pre-work of both fiction and nonfiction pieces, please don't believe that any of these are a "one and done" scenario. Don't fool yourself into thinking you can slot "Pre-work for my novel" on your calendar as a brief afternoon chore. This will take time and energy, as also mentioned earlier. The sense of humor is the manna that will sustain your spirit while you wrestle with the reality of how onerous the pre-work process can be.

How you conduct your pre-work is entirely up to you. Many authors get the entire text laid out-- at least a preliminary version-- before they start writing. Others may find that they've organized them into a good space to write a particular section right this second, which they can edit back in once they've got a final structure in place. Use the method that works best for you. This isn't strictly a knitting project or a quilting project; instead, writing is "the art of letting the muse soar brightly," as a former mentor of mine put it. For your first piece, you may wish to tinker around with your order of operations and structure as you discover what works best for you and your train of thought.

Each book you write will involve a certain amount of experimentation. While doing the pre-work will help you prepare for writing a book, don't feel that everything you've done is carved in stone. As mentioned earlier, you may change some very important details in your book as it develops on the page whether you're writing a fiction piece or a work of nonfiction. When things change, don't feel that you've failed in your pre-work, or that these outlines and hours of research were all in vain. If anything, learning what you don't want to do with your book makes it that much more satisfying when you discover the direction you prefer to take instead.

Whether you end up following these steps exactly or using them as the basis for your own unique process, keep in mind that the goal here is to provide you with direction for your new project. Many first-time authors become frustrated early in the writing process, simply because they haven't done sufficient work ahead of time. The great news is that you can always stop what you're doing mid-sentence, and leave yourself a bookmark or note to return and revisit your notes. Maybe your character map wasn't quite as accurate as you had envisioned. Maybe your angle is slightly askew. Revisit. Regroup. Relax.

You may feel like the pre-work is never-ending, especially if you find yourself revisiting and regrouping more than once. That's not a bad thing at all. It's simply preparing you for the next step of the process, which is setting sail on this monumental voyage. The next step, of course, is to sit down and write a book.

Chapter Three

Surviving The Writing Process

To write a book, begin in a comfortable seated position. Make sure you have a laptop, computer, device, pen and paper, quill and scroll, or whatever media in which you wish to write handy. Close your eyes. Take a deep breath. Exhale slowly. Open your eyes. Write a book. The end.

If only it were that simple! In truth, there will be days when writing comes as naturally to you as breathing or swallowing. On other days, you'll feel nauseated just knowing that the written word exists. There have been times when I've been irked by the label on a packet of snacks simply because it dared to include words and sentences.

The term "surviving" may seem a little dramatic or hyperbolic, but I find that writing is an activity of survival for the author and the piece equally. If you give up on writing your book, then the story does not live on. Equally, if you become so frustrated with the process that you swear off writing anything more significant than your name on a birthday card, your development of passion and talent has terminated. While writing a book is unlikely to be fatal, the knocks you feel during the process might bring an end to the whole endeavor entirely. If you quit, it shouldn't be because continuing would ruin your life, but because you've tried writing, and it's simply not for you.

As always, you'll need time, energy, and a sense of humor, which will apply to the various skills that will help you retain your passion for this project even as the days drag on and words start to lose their meaning. In the following chapters, we'll look at some of the things that help writers retain the desire to write, even if the words aren't coming. They may seem a bit obvious at first, but when you're facing a blank white page, the urge to panic is very strong, especially during your inaugural attempt.

In this section, we'll explore some of the best ways to not panic, stay focused, and keep our eyes on the prize of completing that very first book.

Staying Organized

While it's true that the concept of organization has been mentioned more than a few times already, it really can't be mentioned enough when outlining the process of writing your first book.

The temptation to just open a journal or online word-processing document and start writing will be strong. I highly recommend you follow this urge from time to time, especially when creativity or passion starts waning. The only downfall to this method is that when writing with our eyes closed, we tend to lose sight of where we were trying to go in the first place. This is a great way to get the words flowing, but you might also produce a whole bunch of drivel.

One technique for helping yourself stay accountable when going on these writing sprints involves a little extra organization. Each time you sit down to write, I encourage you to take a few moments to read what you wrote in your previous session. Take a look at your notes, referencing your character map and plot outline for fiction pieces, or glancing back to the final draft of your table of contents for nonfiction writers.

A book, with its thousands of words and hundreds of pages, is overwhelming. It's a long journey full of twists and turns and points and counterpoints. So, try to think of it as an adventure with a destination that's still far in the distance. Imagine you're going to drive a car from Seattle, Washington to Boca Raton, Florida. That's a trip of approximately 3,200 miles, which is approximately 48 hours of continuous driving. Looking at it like that, it seems incredibly overwhelming to take on a trip like that, and you might immediately start looking for the fastest and least expensive flight.

But instead of looking at it as two days of endless driving, remember your humanity. You'll need to stop every so often to eat, fuel up the car, and use the restroom. It's in your best interest to pause once in a while to get a bit of rest, lest your eyes glaze over and your brain goes on auto-pilot. Therefore, it is far more likely that you'll break up the voyage into small, manageable pieces. You'll drive for a few hours the first day, and see how the car is handling. Stop for fuel when you need it, and pop into the station for a drink or snack. Pause at rest areas to use the facilities, walk around a little bit, and maybe take a little nap.

Once you relax and let yourself absorb the beauty of the journey itself, you'll start enjoying it more. Maybe you'll stop at a restaurant that you've always wanted to try. You might choose to wander through town a bit while you're there, dashing into the shops or a little local flavor. Of course, there might be days when it rains, or you're just not feeling the spirit of adventure when you just want to put the pedal to the metal and get on with it, but that's part of the journey, too.

As someone who has made several cross-continental voyages and written just as many books (including a book that I wrote while driving the entirety of the American East Coast), I'm always struck by how similar both processes are. The only major difference is that you can write a book in a stationary position, without leaving the house.

When you open your journal or device and gaze upon that blank page, don't think about how monumental this task is. Don't think about how long it will take you to reach your goal, or how inconvenient it's going to be to make the trip. Instead, break it down into small pieces, just like you would on your road trip.

On your first day of writing, focus on the introduction. Don't overthink it-- just start driving. Tune out the part of your brain that's screaming "This is madness! This is too big! This is going to take too long! You're out of your element!" Lock your mental GPS on the first point you want to make in your book and go for it.

Your introduction is going to set the tone for your book, and if you've created loads of notes during your pre-work, it will be the most honest and forthright thing you write. You haven't had the time to come up with preconceived notions about what you're writing. You haven't developed your voice entirely; you're just pecking along, trying to explain what you're about to write to a reader who has no idea you're even writing a book. The whole process is a mystery at this point. Good thing you have plenty of notes.

Just as you certainly wouldn't attempt to drive from Seattle to Boca Raton without GPS, an atlas, a compass, or some type of tool to help you find the way, the notes you assembled during your pre-work are going to act as a map to guide you through your book. Use this map to help you find your way point-by-point, just as you would make your way across the United States stop-by-stop. Perhaps today you write through Chapter 1, or the point in the plot where the main character is introduced. The next time you sit down, you'll get through Chapter 2, or take the main character to the point where the main conflict is revealed.

Set some very specific points, and write each day until you've completed that portion of your journey. What will make this strategy work, of course, is your ongoing commitment to the organization. When you use a GPS or map to plan a road trip, you plot out your points. You check the roads and get a feel for the highways and byways you need to take to get to your next checkpoint. You don't look to your final destination; you take your time finding your way. You stay with your map at all times. Sure, you might end up following a detour, or discover a more scenic route, but you have a specific place towards which you are heading.

Your pre-work, research, and any notes you make along the way are your map. They tell you where you should go next. Let them do their job. Don't leave your notes in a drawer, decide you were out of your mind and throw them away, or tell yourself you can fly without a map. Once you get into a good flow, you might not need your notes every moment, but given that each session of writing is nearly always different from the day before, there will come a time when you'll deeply crave those notes again.

One particular trick that has saved me a lot of time and tears is to keep a writing journal. You might be thinking "I'm already writing, and you want me to write some more? You're out of your mind." It does sound like overkill, I'll admit. But the purpose of a writing journal can be very simple-- to make notes of what you do each day when writing.

By "journal," I don't necessarily mean a bound notebook type of thing, though that system does tend to work for many writers, especially those early in their careers. careersn use a system of comments and highlight text in a word processing program, or actual sticky notes if you're handwriting your manuscript. Whatever it takes for you to recognize, record, and revisit points in the process where you had to pause to think about things is as fine a method as any, because you're not keeping a writing journal for anyone but yourself.

Writing is not necessarily a chronological thing, even if the piece you are writing is very strictly chronologically structured. You might be knee-deep in Chapter 12, only to realize that life is going to be a lot easier for your characters if you go back and change something slightly in Chapter 3. On the nonfiction front, you might discover that an argument you made in a previous section was weak where it was sitting, and you clearly need to relocate it to a later section, where it actually enhances the discussion. When you make changes like these, make note of them in your writing journal. Examples of these notes might include things like:

"1, February: Changed April's hair color to brown, starting in Chapter 5. Had her dye it so Rebel doesn't recognize her in Chapter 8."

Or in Nonfiction terms:

"25, October: Moved 'Billy the Kid's horse, etc...' from Section 3: Livestock to Section 7: Tradeable Wares. The livestock section now focuses on cattle and farm life. Chickens going under trade as well, though mentioning them in the "Marketable Goods" section of the Livestock section."

The goal of these notes, and the journal as a whole, is that will help you not only recognize changes you made in your draft but will also help you remember *why* you did that in the first place. Sure, you can set up your word processing software to track all changes, but it can't capture your internal argument as you try to make a decision.

The concept of organization extends beyond the notes and to the mental notes and dialogue you're having with yourself as you write your book. There will come times when you type out an entire page, then freeze and think "Is that even what I wanted to say?" Being organized in both your notes and your thought process will help you sort out what you're doing. Being able to remain in synchrony with yourself through the days, months, and years it may take you to write a book is the only way I can think of to continue your productivity through thick and thin.

Being Productive

The original title of this chapter was "Staying on Deadline." In my mind, I was going to explain to you how to budget time to get your first draft done within a specific timeframe. But, as I've preached to you frequently throughout this text, changes do happen.

Instead of teaching you how to force yourself to write when your brain says "no" but the calendar says "yes," I'd rather encourage you to develop a passion for productivity. Truly talented writers can spirit up an entire text from nothing in a matter of seconds, but that's not the experience you should have for your first book. Rather, your first book should be an effort you undertake because you truly want to. It should be positive and passionate, and whether or not you choose to ever write another book, you should walk away from the process proud of yourself for having done something so monumental.

You should set a timeline for yourself, as I mentioned earlier, simply to keep your brain aware of the fact that this is a real thing, and it does deserve your attention. How strict you are with your deadline depends on how well you know yourself. Some of us need the pressure to thrive, which means being a little aggressive with deadlines to keep ourselves focused and excited about our writing. On the other hand, you might avoid excess anxiety by allowing yourself generous milestones that simply demonstrate you are making forward motion, rather than wallowing in each potential sticky spot.

Regardless of your expectations, the main goal of setting a timeline is to promote writing. When writing our first book, nearly every writer I've spoken to says the same thing: We start obsessing about whether it's good, interrupt ourselves, rewrite the same paragraph eight times, give up because it's too hard, wonder if we're failures at everything we try, spiral into self-doubt, and basically have a very bad time. Instead of making it good on the first pass, just concentrate on making it.

You want to write a good book, but before it can be good, it must be a book. Write it. Just write the blessed thing! Just like you'd step on the gas and speed away from a roach-infested hotel room on a cross-country road trip, sometimes it's best to keep moving forward and not look back when writing.

Make adjustments. Pay attention to detours. Take the scenic route. But don't spend too much time glancing back at where you've been until you really know where you're going. If you're going along at a nice clip in the introductory pages and suddenly remember that April's hair is going to change color, don't stop. Use that writing journal to make note of it, and keep going. There might be a reason why your brain wanted you to write it this way now. Explore that, but make note of it, in case you don't like where that path leads. You wouldn't turn off your GPS when you got lost, and you shouldn't stop where you are, turn off the car, and call it quits, either. You can always come back when you have more time and fuel.

Remember as you write that when you come back later, you'll have a fuller grasp of what (if anything) needs to be changed. You could go back on April's hair throughout the entire book. What if you discover, just as you're wrapping things up, that April really enjoys changing her hair color, and she does it a few times throughout the tale in order to be more of a social chameleon? You've just realized that you need to revisit every mention of April's hair color to make sure it fits the social situation in that scene. Things like this happen, so make notes and come back later; go forward for now.

You'll also need to examine your relationship with the word "progress." Earlier, we discussed how the recommended 2000 words each day might not make sense for you, at least not daily. I encourage you to gauge progress not by how many words you write each day, but by the things you actually accomplish when you do sit down to write. If you only write 100 words, but you manage to get yourself through a section that was particularly troublesome for you, that's progress! If you do a 4000-word sprint because you haven't had the time to sit down and write for yourself in weeks, that's also progress!

Many people get a little frenzied during their first attempt to write something substantial. If discipline helps you thrive, then by all means, create a stringent program for yourself. I find that if my deadlines are too far in the future, I will almost dare myself to wait until the last minute. But, if I choose instead to force myself to make some form of progress each day, I procrastinate less and I love my final product more. That being said, giving myself a very specific quantity of words to accomplish each time I sit down would exacerbate my anxiety. I'm more of the "write until your head is empty" type of writer when I have my druthers. Writing in a professional capacity has helped me learn how to hold myself more accountable to a schedule, but hopefully, your first book won't come with a tight deadline!

In preparing for your first book, though, you may not really know what your style is like. You may have never sat down and written thousands of words at once, or if you have, it may have been long, long ago. It's not the type of thing everyone gets to enjoy in their personal or professional life, so it may feel very strange at first.

In fact, it might quite literally feel strange, as in physically uncomfortable. If you're not familiar with typing, your fingers and wrists might become sore or achy after a particularly long stretch of typing. Handwriting your book can also lead to aches and pains in the wrists and fingers. If you don't usually sit for hours on end, your spine and posterior may start to object to your new pastime.

Keep in mind that writing is actual exercise, for your mind as well as your body. Just as you wouldn't enter a marathon if you've never jogged down your driveway, you'll need to give yourself time to adjust to this new activity, both mentally and physically. You might find yourself feeling exhausted at the end of a writing session, or wired from a burst of endorphins as you try a new task. No one told me about how writing can affect the body, so I was completely surprised when I burst out crying inconsolably for half an hour after submitting my final draft. Your brain will be taxed. You might forget things. You might find yourself on edge. You might find it difficult to sleep or to rise. These are all very real side effects of writing your first book.

Over time, the process will become easier, but you need to train yourself to endure it. Take breaks to avoid actual writer's cramps. I like to get up and walk around the room every thirty minutes or so. I wait until I've reached a good stopping point, of course, but then I close my eyes, do some desk stretches, and get up for a good minute or two. Sitting on an exercise ball instead of a regular chair is a great way to avoid the pitfalls of poor posture when seated. In the Resources section, I've included a few links to exercises you can do to keep your body as limber as your mind during the writing process.

Sometimes, if I find my mind blank, I'll turn to the internet and read something related to my topic, just to get the brain juices going. When I was writing heavily for the automotive community, I would pause work to watch episodes of *Top Gear* or *Rust Valley Restorers* to refresh my appreciation of writing in the right tone and voice. Don't beat your poor brain into submission over this task; instead, let be a part of the instrument and play for the muses naturally. Alternatively, I'll shut off the computer and do some Yoga Nidra to prevent my brain from going into overdrive. Find what helps you think-- I've included a few suggestions for brain-cleansing activities in the Resources section. It's important to cleanse the mind from time to time to keep your mental focus and emotions in check.

Give yourself time to focus on learning your own process. By emphasizing the overall accomplishment of any progress at all, you're giving yourself the room you need to learn your own needs. Your procedures will start to fall into place as you become more familiar with your mental, emotional, and physical needs. Make adjustments. I can't tell you how many playlists I auditioned before I found the exact tunes I need to be productive.

Seasoned authors across the board recommend finding a good place in which you can do your writing. A quiet spot, where no one can bother you and you don't find yourself tempted by too many distractions can be incredibly helpful in inspiring and maintaining productivity. This doesn't mean you need to build yourself a state-of-the-art office unless you truly want to. Many a bestseller has been written at a kitchen table, behind a blanket "wall" in the living room, on a closet floor, or in the dark once the kids have gone to sleep. Part of finding your groove is finding a good place to work. If you find yourself being very easily distracted, move. Set yourself up for success; trying to "push through" a situation that just isn't working will only bring distaste for the overall experience.

Over time, your progress will become a process, and your process will in turn raise your productivity. The muscles that ached and the tears that were shed will all become more rare, as your body learns to sit and the mind becomes accustomed to this exciting task. You'll feel less forced, frantic, and formal and more focused. You'll look forward to your writing time. Knowing that you'll return to a sort of normalcy or even a state of bliss after that first major road bump of entering unfamiliar territory should help you keep your eyes on the prize, so to speak. Travel one stop at a time, but if you remind yourself that you're moving forward, the journey will be all the more enjoyable and rewarding once you've reached its end.

Dealing with Changes

By now, you might be a little confused about the methods I'm pre-scribing for you: always go forward, except when you turn around and go back, but always make notes about why you did then, then go forward again. That's a pretty accurate description of the writing process, but since this is your first time, I'll try to simplify it a bit.

Always go forward. Progress is good. Write more words, make more of your book appear before you, continue the momentum, and so forth. The more you write, the greater the chance that you'll work yourself through those moments of confusion and self-doubt. Always end the session with more words than when you started.

However, change is inevitable. We must not fear change. You will wake up one morning and realize that you didn't include a certain detail earlier, and you need to add it. Do just that. Note it in your journal, and then continue forward. Don't spend an excessive amount of time re-reading what you've already done, because you've got an entire revision and editing process for that. When you go back to make essential changes, I strongly encourage you to put blinders on to the rest of what you've written, at least for the moment. Make your change, make sure it exists peacefully with the surrounding text, and then return to the prospect of forward motion.

But the concept of "change" isn't strictly limited to parts already written. As you move ever boldly forward, get ready for things to get weird. Your characters may turn out to be totally different from your first impressions. You may find that something you considered irrefutable truth was proven incorrect recently. In this great journey of writing, there will be roadblocks and detours you never intended to take.

So how do you deal with unexpected change, especially when you're supposed to be the one in control here? This is one of the very few scenarios in which I would encourage you, as a writer, to pause briefly. The other scenarios include natural disasters, fire, and medical emergencies, but this is one of the few instances when you have a free pass to stop yourself before you proceed past the point of no return. If you have discovered a major gap in reality, you have permission to stop and regroup.

By "major gap in reality," I am referencing situations in fictional pieces such as but not limited to:

- Your character's personality has changed so drastically, they cannot realistically perform the plot as drafted

- The survival of a character is dependent on your decisions, and you hadn't initially planned to write a mortal departure

- You're reaching the ending far sooner than you expected

- The original ending you planned is completely unlikely

- The genre skipped track on you, and in order to follow the new version, you need to do more research

For nonfiction writers, you might encounter the following, and then some:

- Your main argument is based on a fact that has been proven false

- In writing a particular section, you discovered you have a very unequal distribution of information compared to the rest of the sections

- You're making the same point and argument repeatedly, but not in an informative manner

- You're bleeding a rock with your resources

- Your interviewees stop responding to you, and now you have absolutely no idea how their story ends

As you can see, these are not mere "situations," but occurrences that would require major edits to everything that you have written and will continue to write. Think of it as a subconscious railroad switch, gently guiding your barreling train to another track without missing a beat. You may have thought you were the engineer of this particular train, but surprise! Something happened along the way, and you're in an entirely different place.

This does not necessarily mean you should jump ship and abandon your work. In each case, you can revise the text to suit the new situation, if you feel it is for the better. That means you'll have to revisit your initial plans as well as the developing text in order to find all of the bits that are impacted by this update. Sometimes, you'll find that you can actually tie it all together simply by moving forward. For example, in a situation where my interviewees ghosted me, I was able to take the information they had given me in our first sessions, flip the hypothesis of the article, adjust my gaze a bit, and create an even more interesting article because of my changes. Don't give up. Don't be shocked. Look at your piece and think, "What can I make that's even better?"

But sometimes, you're completely blindsided by the change. You can't understand why a particular character comes across as cruel and narcissistic, because you've always intended her to be the self-sacrificing character. Your heroine is annoying, and it seems like the characters are less and less interested in the rising action each day. In the nonfiction world, you might discover you're practically shouting your text, trying to impress upon your reader how important this detail is, or you're repeating phrases verbatim unintentionally. You might look at your book in utter fear, wondering how on Earth did this happen? Who wrote this?

First, know that this is very natural. It can be a bit unsettling when you look at something you've produced, and it is very much not like you expected it at all. Sometimes what our mind's eye sees is completely exempt from replication in the real world, especially when we add our own perspective to it. It sounds a little scary or supernatural, but the way you feel in your own world can very easily be reflected in what you write. Have you ever cleaned the house angrily, or washed the dishes when you were really happy? The way we feel has a lot to do with how we act, and when the duty at hand is translating your own imagination into the written word... well, a funny thing happened on the way to the paper.

The more you write, the easier it will be to avoid this phenomenon, because you'll recognize how you write when you're mad, sad, lonely, anxious, or slightly tipsy on white wine. There will be subtle changes in your style, and the developments in your text will start to reflect the way you're reacting in real life. We write what we know, and if you're having a bad day, you'll use your characters as a sounding board, or your arguments might become a little more impassioned.

This is another reason why I recommend you keep moving forward as much as possible. The energy you bring to the pages when you write is important for productivity, and it can become very stagnant as you continue forward. If you're dealing with something in your private life, keep writing, even if your original concepts change. Likewise, there will be chapters that bore you. Push forward through this to see what comes out on the other side. Your energy is what will keep a book churning forward. When you stop this energy from lingering too long on something that's already been done, you lose forward momentum. Your energy changes. The moment is lost. See where things go, and if it turns out that the inadvertent turn at the station wasn't for the best, first decide where you can go along this route.

When it comes to writing your first book, something will inevitably change. It may be the contents of the book, or it may be your own perspective. Don't fear change; follow it. And when it becomes clear that you need to reassess, do so. What you build upon your current structure is only going to be better for it. But for the love of everything, make notes about it so you don't lose your train of thought or the steam to continue.

Perhaps this was not the outline of "the writing process" you wanted. You might have been looking for someone to help you put one word after the other. Maybe you wanted to know what the best adjectives are, or how to really use adverbs to spice up your writing. Those are very important things to know as a writer, after all!

While I don't disagree that writing is art with words, I also don't feel like I should be telling you how to execute your art. There is a lot about writing to me-- and to many others who write for a living-- that is still somewhat spiritual or sacred. I don't know why I love doing it. I don't know why it's always come so easily to me. I can't tell you where my brain goes, where the words come from, or how I know exactly how I want to organize things. When a character is engaged in dialogue, I don't know who is really speaking to whom on a subconscious level. What I do know is that I can't imagine a way to force someone to let their brain flow into the written word. You just have to accept that it is your task and try it.

And that, more than anything, is my main piece of writing advice: Try it. Don't look at what you've written and say, "Oh that's crap, and I'll never get better." The first time isn't meant to be good. The first few pages will be awkward. You'll be able to see the cracks where you might've stumbled and fudged it for a little bit because you weren't quite sure what was happening. Maybe you got hyper-aware and self-conscious and started doing the literary equivalent of stammering. That's OK! That happens all the time! In fact, that's exactly what the editing stage is for.

If you are expecting to produce Nobel-winning content the first time you even try to write, then I formally invite you to get over yourself. Write first, then perfection. Make the book, then make the book better. I'm not saying be lazy-- always give it your best effort and as much energy as you can muster-- but recognize that you are actually expected to go back and make changes.

In the next chapter, we'll learn how "edit" is not a "four-letter word," despite the fact that it does contain four letters. Change is good. Edits are expected. You have an opportunity to clean the entire house before your company comes over, so take advantage of it.

Chapter Four

The Editing Stage

According to Merriam-Webster's online dictionary:

Definition of **Edit**

transitive verb

1a: To prepare (something, such as literary material) for publication or public presentation

edit a manuscript

b: to assemble (something, such as a moving picture or tape recording) by cutting and rearranging

edit a film

c: to alter, adapt, or refine especially to bring about conformity to a standard or to suit a particular purpose

carefully edited the speech

Edit a data file

As you read that, you may see that there is nothing in there linking editing to being a worthless writer. Because it's not true. Editing isn't necessary because you're a terrible person who deserves nothing good; editing is an opportunity to make sure what you've written is exactly right.

Somehow, there has grown a perceived notion that editing is bad, and only people who aren't very good at writing make edits. This is, of course, nonsense. If you care enough to swallow your pride, abandon your ego, and re-read everything you've written to make it even better, then you clearly care deeply about your book and want it to be the best it can be.

Also, for those for whom the reality hasn't quite set in yet: Congratulations; you've written a book.

When you reach the editing process, you have officially written a book. Now you get to make it a good book, and you shouldn't view that as punishment for not writing a book perfectly the first time through, but as a privilege for following your passion and making this dream come true in the first place. If you can grind through the long and emotional process of writing the book, then certainly you can go through the thing again with a feather duster and a bit of polish!

Remember: writing a book requires time, energy, and a sense of humor. It is in your best interest to extend these traits through the editing process as well. Let's take a look at some other things to keep in mind when entering and proceeding through the editing phase of your book. And remember: it's just a phase!

How to Ignore Your Instincts and Edit Subjectively

It is all too common to get that sinking-pit stomach feeling when you face the editing phase. You are going to come face to face with your own human fallibility, after all. It's one thing to emotionally prepare for the act of editing, but to actually do the chore is another thing altogether.

There are two typical reactions to facing the emotions that come with the first round of editing of your first book:

1. Tear it apart. Tear it all apart. Burn it down and start over.

2. Put it in a box. Lock it. Throw away the key. Bury the box.

Neither of these are going to help you. Therefore, you need to learn how to ignore your instincts and simply edit your book.

There are different ways of going about it. If you've been keeping a writing journal, one of the first things you can do is read the journal, and then look back at all the parts you've referenced. Make sure April's hair is the correct color at all times. Be certain that Billy the Kid's horse isn't running amok throughout the text. If you changed a plot point or argument in the mid-to-late part of the book, make sure all earlier references have been updated, as well. For those using a word processing program, the "Find" feature can come in very handy here.

Readers can forgive a lot of things and suspend their disbelief significantly, but inconsistencies are just annoying. Avoid annoying your reader. Do a read-through of your book with the specific intention of making sure everything is consistent from chapter to chapter. And by "everything," I truly mean everything. Here are a few examples of things to check for when evaluating the consistency of your text:

- Is your tone and voice the same throughout the book, or did that energy from being in a different mood leak through, as I mentioned it might?

- Does the narrator or point of view of the text remain the same?

- Are all mentions of locations or settings accurate (this is equally important for fiction and nonfiction works)?

- Are all names spelled the same way throughout the text, or are annotations made where names may change purposefully? (Example: Referencing members of royalty is one situation in which individuals may have a given name, a familial nickname, one or more titular names, and so on. Let the readers know all of them, so it's not confusing when you switch between them.)

- Are all personal details, such as outward appearance, clothing/style, personality, and other identifying characteristics unchanging, OR do these details change appropriately at the right time and remain changed until otherwise specified?

- Does your treatment of various issues or scenarios align throughout the book?

- Is there anything you mention at some point in your introduction or thesis that immediately disappears?

Essentially, you want to read through your book and not once think, "Wait, what happened to ___." Whether that blank is filled by an important historical reference, a character name, a recognizable tattoo, a dog, an interviewee, a significant resource, or a portion of your argument, don't let it dangle.

So how do you clean it up? Start with evaluation. Do you really need that thing that fills the blank to exist in the first place? What type of effort in the form of rewrites will be needed to re-establish consistency? While you may find that you can get rid of the offending disagreeable detail, it may be salvageable. You may, in fact, find that taking the time to do some pretty sizable rewrites to explain the inconsistency will not only eliminate confusion but bolster your work altogether. Nearly every writer has had a cringe-worthy moment where they discovered a major boo-boo or blunder, only to write it into the text with great success.

Once you've got a thorough and complete text without any strange wandering threads that lead nowhere, it's time to address the language and grammar. If you're using a word processing program, you'll likely have minimal typos, unless you happen to make typos that actually make sense. I really need to send my editors a fruit basket at some point, because they have caught me in the act of things that legitimately don't make sense. After all, Google Docs autocorrected my typos to something similar but not right. You'll want to find those before you release your book to the outside world. Even if you never intend your text to see wide distribution, you do want to avoid hearing every person who does read the book say "Did you know that on page 113, you used the word 'lighting' instead of 'lightning?'" And yes, that is a real example from my own career-- the error appeared in a commemorative handbook for a one-time event, and I may never recover.

At this point, you have uncovered and corrected all glaring errors and omissions. If this is a low-stakes project, you may wish to press forward and pursue distribution of your project now, whether that means printing up booklets for your friends or family or sending off a file to your loved ones. However, if you want to make a big splash with your first book, it's time to call in an outside party to read and evaluate your text. Sounds scary? It's absolutely terrifying, at least the first few times. But having a beta reader or editing team tear your book to bits is far less dehumanizing than reading negative reviews. Trust me.

The Importance of Outside Readers

If you're concerned about letting other people read your work, imagine how I'm feeling right now. I'm writing a chapter about editing that will be edited by my long-suffering editors. Talk about working under pressure!

The truth of the matter is that I, personally, am thrilled when my work goes off to editors and beta readers. I feel like I write in a vacuum, typing out things that only I might ever want to read, so having a clean-up crew to make what I write suitable for public consumption is a major relief to me. In fact, if a manuscript comes back without being shredded, redlined, and annotated, I become paranoid that I've done something wrong.

The purpose of an editor is to catch what you've missed. An ideal editor should have a strong background in language and grammar, and understand the various current formats for both fiction and non-fiction pieces. I went to school in the 1980s. The styles we used back then are long gone, and the grammar guides that led to my high marks in literature and writing are now laughably out of date. I try to keep up, but then I throw out a super-casual, candid, conversational book like this one, and my poor editors suffer trying to make it fit a format. And I would like to note that I am very, very sorry for their suffering, even though they'll likely remove one of those "very" for being redundant.

Beta readers, on the other hand, are there to make sure your text works. They can provide editing and formatting corrections as necessary, but the primary goal of a beta reader is to make sure that the book works before anyone sees it. Much like a trusted friend evaluating your hair, makeup, and outfit before you leave the house for an important shindig, the beta reader ensures your slip isn't showing and there isn't lipstick on your teeth, metaphorically speaking.

The purpose of an editor or beta reader is to approach your book objectively, without any bias or preconceived notion. Therefore, you may not want a close friend, housemate, or partner to be your first reader, unless they are very good at separating the art from the artist. What I mean by that is this: someone who knows you very well will know your tone of voice, how you communicate, and even the subconscious nuances of the way you speak and think. They'll read your book in your voice, which will be beneficial for them, but not every reader will have that same understanding of your style.

If an editor or beta reader has done a very thorough job, they'll share their own insight into what they like about your book, and what didn't work for them. I strongly encourage you to consider this informa-tion. With a few exceptions, they aren't sharing their thoughts and recommendations to be mean, but rather because they have discovered opportunities for making your book even stronger. Let your soul and your ego rest peacefully, knowing that this isn't an attack, but rather an invitation from a like-minded friend to make things even better than they are.

It is very easy, as a writer, to write from your own point of view and understanding about a topic. Unfortunately, that makes assumptions about what the reader already knows and understands. Very rarely are these things universal. Therefore, when an editor or beta reader points out that the jump from point to point doesn't make sense, don't bother thinking "No one understands me as a writer," but rather, "What can I do to make this clearer to my audience?" Remember that you're trying to create a clear picture of your intentions, regardless of whether you're writing fiction or nonfiction. Clarity is the best way to get your reader on board, so if those who are reading the book are having trouble following, it doesn't mean you're a horrible writer, but merely that you have some explaining to do.

I realize that can be a big jolt to the ego, especially when you've tried your best and it's your first effort. But before you begin licking your wounds and avowing you'll never write again, pause for a moment and really read the comments you've received from your outside reader. It is very possible that they simply weren't the right readers for the assignment. It is also possible that they headed into it with a very different concept of what they were supposed to be doing. Any editor or beta reader worth their salt will leave a slew of comments and feedback about your work. You'll be able to tell from reading them not only what they objectively thought, but what they expected from your work, as well. Sometimes-- however unintentional it may be-- what they want your book to be will differ from what's on the page, which will lead to a whole avalanche of misunderstanding and lack of appreciation.

One way to mitigate this is to do a trial run with your outside reader. Send them a few pages. A chapter. See what they do with it. If they come back to you with feedback that makes sense, then you've got a good match, and you should run with it. Let them have at it and build a better book. Alternatively, if they clearly missed the point of the assignment, perhaps they should wait for the final product. They may be wonderful, perfectly intelligent people, but just as you wouldn't want to listen to an entire album in a musical style you loathe, forcing someone to read a book they just don't get is equally unfair, and no one will benefit from it. While you want your book to have the greatest appeal possible, truly nothing in this world is beloved by all... not even cheese.

My last piece of advice when it comes to working with editors beta readers and outside parties of all kinds is this: You don't always have to take their advice. At the end of the day, this is your book, filled with your ideas, research, time, energy, and sense of humor. At some point, you will need to decide for and by yourself that the book you have created is exactly the product you intended in the first place.

And that part is tough enough that it gets its own chapter.

When to Call It "Done"

When I was a young person, studying writing at school, I hated what our professor called "rewind weeks." That week, instead of submitting a brand new piece for peer review and group discussion, we were to take a previous piece and make it new again. Hardly anyone liked it. One fellow, in particular, would do something delightfully subservient, like change a single character's appearance in a way that really didn't matter to the context of the story and leave everything else the same. One writer enjoyed rewriting his work so that the letter "e" wouldn't appear anywhere in the text. The rest of us, however, begrudgingly leafed through our portfolio to figure out what we could unenthusiastically turn into a new piece.

But here's the thing: we were all missing the point of the exercise. The whole reason why we were doing this was to drill home the lesson that any piece you write is going to be a reflection of who, where, what, and how you were at the time you wrote it. When you do massive revisions, it's usually because the version of yourself reading the book is markedly different from the person who wrote it in the first place. While you're welcome to do that, you need to know that you aren't required to do so.

Sometimes, it's best to just let a piece be. There have been many times when writers look at something and say, "That's crap. I'll have the editors deal with it," again, with apologies to my editors. But then the editors take a look at it and feel that it isn't crap at all. That's because we're our own worst critics, and we won't let things leave our grasp while we can still control everything about them. Sounds psychologically deep, but many of us are hardwired to be absolute control monsters, and that's okay.

Letting go of a manuscript is hard. I genuinely cried the first time I submitted a final draft, as I mentioned before. I was equal parts proud of myself, relieved that the process was done, and terrified that I had just unleashed a bunch of garbage on the literary community. The truth is that most of the things that are written will be sublimely enjoyed by many people, while others just don't care for it very much... just like cheese.

This does not mean you're a failure. Negative feedback and de-structive criticism have nothing to do with you or your talents. If someone truly cares, they'll leave you constructive feedback and notes that can help you build upon themselves. Otherwise, they're just miserable people who want the world to know they've had an awful time.

Think of your favorite musical artist. Do you know how many people hate their work? Bach, Beethoven, The Beatles, Beck... for each of these artists there is someone out there who hates everything they've done with a passion so deep they could choke on it. But that doesn't mean they aren't talented and don't deserve their careers. It means there's someone who just doesn't like them.

So, when you receive harsh words about your book-- whether they're from someone else or your own brain-- let it go. It's one book in a vast universe of books. It's one literary experience. At some point, you have to stop picking at it and just let it live the way it was intended.

That doesn't mean you have to completely tune out any feedback about the book. If something is universally confusing, then it might need some patient tinkering. But if people just don't like it, then they can donate it or put it in a garage sale. Everyone in this world has albums, movies, books, and even clothing that they once loved, but now realize they bought in error. The world keeps turning.

Earlier in this book, I mentioned how you do need to do some things for readers, such as make an intelligible book. That courtesy does not extend to making sure they absolutely adore the book. At the dawn of my career, I edited and beta read for a person whose books were truly appalling to me. His characters were racist, there was a sexual assault of some kind in each chapter, and I simply couldn't follow the plot lines at all because I was so emotionally triggered. I came to realize that I was just not the best beta reader for his books, and we parted ways amicably. Guess who's working with a team to develop his work for television. Everything has an audience. Don't find inspiration in the harsh words of the naysayers; grow with those who already know you're capable.

So, now that you've learned that you can always change things and no one's going to like everything anyway, including yourself, that leaves the question that started this chapter: How do you know when your book is done?

The very textbook, fact-based answer is that your book is done once you've reached a point where you're confident that it fully reflects all of the intentions you outlined in your pre-work. Though things changed during the pre-work and the writing itself, the general idea of writing a decent book on a specific topic should still be the bulls-eye you've been aiming for all along. If each page makes sense and contributes something to the overall book and reader experience, then you're done. Save file. Submit. Print. Whatever you plan to do with your completed book, now is the time to do it. Have a toast, call your friends, cry... whatever it takes to release all of the emotions and stress you've built along the road.

The esoteric version of this is that you'll simply know. Sometimes, you'll get through a round of edits and just know that your book is ready to fly. Alternatively, you'll be so sick of looking at it that you don't care if it flops, as long as it gets off of your desktop. Realistically, the logic behind these feelings is the knowledge within yourself that there is simply nothing else you can do to make the book any more ready than it is at that moment. But the romantic notion of understanding your book on a spiritual level is a bit more fun than really digging into the psychology of it.

If you are going to publish your book on a public level, beyond distribution to your inner circle, this is not the end of the line. You can certainly cheer, cry, and celebrate, but there may still be some work to be done on your end. Read on to determine how-- and if-- you want your book to see the light of day.

Chapter Five

A Brief Word About Publishing

Years ago, publishing a piece meant sending it off to be printed in a bound book format with shiny covers and real pages that could be rudely dog-eared. With the advent of the household printer, it became easier to print off entire pieces without them ever passing the threshold, though it's difficult to say that using a household printer was ever "easy." Paper jams, impossible toner levels, and the cost of printer paper made it a less than enjoyable process, but nonetheless, one anyone with the right equipment could complete.

Today, there are many paths to publication on a variety of scales. The difficulty, stress, and rewards for each method are very different and should be thoroughly considered before throwing all of your proverbial eggs in one proverbial basket.

Each of the methods for getting published that I'll mention is worthy of its own book, but I'm going to skim over each for now. There are several reasons for this. First, I don't want anyone to feel that publishing is mandatory. Writing for pleasure is still very much a real thing, and I want anyone attempting to write a book to feel like this can be our little secret. Next, the publishing world is so volatile, that I couldn't possibly do it justice without writing a lengthy volume. Furthermore, the methods are constantly changing and may be different from location to location, person to person, or website to website. It's a very nuanced business, so rather than provide you with any details that might be inaccurate, I'll instead give you the basics and point you in the direction of more authoritative information.

Ghost Writing

Ghostwriting is a term used to describe a situation where one party hires another party to write about a particular topic on their behalf. Many people are looking for ghostwriters, especially those looking for someone to capture in the written word their own advice or life story. As a new writer, this can be beneficial because someone else is guiding you, and that dangling paycheck just beyond the deadline can be a great incentive... as long as you're confident that you can follow through with the commitment.

Pros:

- All you have to do is write and edit

- No politics, no agents

- You'll likely get paid

- If the book tanks, no one knows it was you who wrote it

Cons:

- You usually do not get to choose the topic

- The person requesting the writing may have very specific

requirements, including a deadline

- No commission

- If the book performs extremely well, no one knows it was you who wrote it

Self Publishing

There are many venues out there for self-publishing your book, so take the time to explore your options to find the best fit for you and your goals. In this method of publication, you hire editors and designers to format your book, then submit it for publication through a business that strictly prints your book to order. Many publication venues have a minimum number of physical books they'll print at a time, but self-published ebooks are extremely popular.

Pros:

- You can print anything, anytime

- You don't have to print millions of copies

- You can earn a commission, depending on the distribution method or site you use

- You can make changes to your book at any time since they are printed to order. Just make sure you're using the latest file for future publications

Cons:

- You'll need to have design skills, or higher someone to ensure it's formatted correctly for publishing or ebook distribution

- You will not see your face smiling back at you from a book jacket in the window of a bookstore

- You don't commission unless it sells. All marketing and promotion is up to you

- You will need to pay for each copy that is produced, which means you may lose money at first

Finding an Agent/Publisher

Not for the faint of heart or those with low to moderate self-esteem. This is the most political version of getting your work published, but if you're very much interested in becoming a famous author, you'll want to consider finding an agent.

In this model, you send your book to agents who are looking for new material. Agents work on commission; therefore, it is in the best interest of each agent to only take on clients they believe they can sell. If an agent does not believe they can sell your book, they will reject it. Rejection hurts, but it's not personal.

Once you find an agent, the agent will pitch your book to a variety of publishing houses. Again, they will only accept your work if they think they can profit from it. If they don't think there's money in your book, they will reject it.

Eventually, your book will be published. You will be paid royalties, which are a percentage of the profit of your book. Your book will need to sell so many copies to pay for its own publishing, so you will only get paid after your book has "earned out," or paid for itself.

Pros:

- You don't have to pay to publish your own work

- You may be asked to produce multiple books

- Being signed by a publisher is a big deal with significant prestige and honor

- You won't have to do any of the hustling, like marketing, printing, ordering, and design

Cons:

- You may have to relinquish creative control. Always review your contract in detail

- You may be rejected many times before you finally find an agent and publisher

- Your contract may limit your rights to your original work

- You may be forced to do press and signings (which might be a pro if you're into that sort of thing!)

Publishing your work is often a strange juxtaposition of guts and glory. I've included some resources to help you dig further into any options that might sound ideal for you and your goals for your freshly written book.

Prologue

So there you go. That's how you do it. Go write a book.

At this point, you may still feel like you don't entirely know "how" to write a book. I wish I could say that there's a step-by-step process that's super easy to follow and absolutely fail-proof, but there's really not.

Avid readers may recall the journey of a girl named Dorothy Gale along a certain Yellow Brick Road. She had guidance along the way, but there was quite a bit that she had to figure out on her own. At the risk of throwing yet another analogy on the heap, writing a book is a very similar exercise in endurance and perseverance. If you have a general idea of where you're headed and a destination or goal in mind, you'll be very well prepared to handle any bumps in the road that might head your way, whether you realize it or not.

You might feel right now that I haven't possibly addressed every single step, every possible problem or pratfall, and how to get out of it. In fact, I have. Most of the obstacles that try us during the process of writing our first books come from the enemy within us. More than anything, novice writers are typically tripped up and dissuaded from completing big projects because they feel it would be a waste of time. They aren't good enough to write a book. They started a book once, but they lost interest in it. They decided they "sounded dumb," so they gave up. When I ask people how their books are going, and they are not going well at all, these are the types of answers I receive.

What I hope I have impressed upon you, more than anything else, is that you have the power within you to get past these obstacles. Writing a book takes a lot of time, which is why I warned you of that right from the get-out. Time, energy, and a sense of humor are all required to make it through the process of writing a book, whether it's your first or your 101st effort.

You will spend a lot of time writing a book, but whether that time is truly "wasted" is for you to decide. Human beings are very good at finding new and exciting ways to waste time, and frankly, if you felt like you got something from it, emotionally, spiritually, mentally, physically, educationally, or what-have-you, then my personal view is that your time was not "wasted." It was used in an atypical way to provide you with personal enrichment.

As far as whether you're "good enough?" By now, you should be aware that we are all simultaneously good enough and not good enough. Some readers will love it. Some will hate it. The majority of readers will think it's fine and have no major feelings one way or the other about it.

At the beginning of the book, we talked about maintaining realistic expectations for books, and figuring out why we wanted to write them in the first place. Aligning our priorities mentally and emotionally when it comes to undertaking an entire tome is directly related to the level of energy we put into getting the task done. Aim higher than you need to, and you'll put undue pressure on yourself, struggling to write a book and ultimately feeling like you've "failed," which is false. You'll put too much energy in too fast and burn out when you discover the process can take a miserable amount of time and more than basic enthusiasm. As I said then, writing a best seller is a remarkable goal, but don't register for the marathon without jogging a few steps first. You are good enough; you just need to set yourself up to succeed.

And then that sense of humor. At some point, everyone seems to feel like they "sound dumb." I would absolutely love to read more psychological and sociological studies examining why those in creative fields doubt their own abilities and intelligence. In the meantime, I can only speculate and recommend you meditate on these concepts to see if they can help you break through some mental blockages of your own.

When you write, especially if you've never written before, you're using your mind and your body in new ways. It's all very unfamiliar, and sometimes, if you stare at a page or a word too long, you stop recognizing it. Don't let your brain play games with your spirit. A sense of humor will get you far in the writing process.

When you find yourself feeling ignorant or start having negative thoughts about your capabilities, take a break. Go do some research to validate yourself. Read a book from an author you admire. Some writers recommend reading an author in your genre, but I find that leads me down a path of temptation to compare myself to the other author. Let your brain find inspiration without dysfunction-- that is, fill your brain with information that will reignite your passion to pursue this endeavor, without feeding into any negative self-talk.

Always do the pre-work. As time goes by, and you gain more experience, you may find this part of the process going more and more smoothly. After a while, it starts to feel less like work and more like "the fun part." Really let yourself soar when it comes to dreaming up your book, especially in the very first few moments of making it real. Start really, really big, and then let yourself understand your book and where it really needs to go in order to make yourself clear.

In fact, allow yourself to suspend disbelief a bit in these first few days of getting to know your book. I like to really immerse myself in whatever I'm writing about. If it's a particular brand of car, for example, I'll look at pictures, read the history of the manufacturer, and even drive past a dealership lot if I can. When I'm writing a fiction piece, I like to really imagine who each character is. Don't give them arbitrary descriptions; instead, think about how they wear their hair (if they have hair). What's their posture like? How do they move? What do their facial expressions look like? It sounds a little strange at first, but consider how your belief in this new reality that you're creating will help the reader ease more swiftly into your newfound world.

When you finally feel ready to sit down and write, make sure you are really prepared to commit to this undertaking. You're going to feel uncomfortable in every imaginable sense of the word, at least for the first few sessions. Are you prepared to break through the agony to pursue the ecstasies of writing?

Rather than arming you with a gimmick that claims to help new-comers write better, I'm furnishing you with certain truths and ex-pectations that aren't discussed widely, though I'm not sure why the secrecy is so well-maintained. Whenever I mention through the intro-duction that I'm a writer, this detail is more and more frequently met with a self-deprecating joke about how the other party is "practically illiterate," or something along those lines. While I would absolutely love to be validated in my suspicions that I am the most talented beast walking this planet, deep down inside, I know that's not true.

Furthermore, it makes me very sad that so many people have had their confidence completely squelched when it comes to doing some-thing creative. Why are standards so high that no one can simply dabble in art, music, crafting, cooking, or writing without being ex-tremely good at it? You haven't "tried to write a book" if you got three sentences in and decided you were a failure. You weren't. You got overwhelmed. You psyched yourself out. You chose to quit before you had to admit it was uncomfortable and you weren't sure how to deal with that discomfort.

The writing process is truly unlike anything else. While there is some order to things, it's not an exact science, except for some forms of nonfiction. If you prefer detailed instructions, you need to figure them out yourself. Just like the road trip from Seattle to Boca, there are a vast quantity of possible routes. But don't let that be your reason for never making the trip. Maps were made by people taking the trip and figuring out where to go. You'll need to make your own map the first time you make this particular journey, and that can certainly be overwhelming. But think how much more fun the next road trip will be, now that you know the best route.

If anything, I want you to feel empowered by this book to take the plunge and make it through the writing process. You certainly won't arrive at the end unscathed, but I hope that the previous pages of text have helped you understand some of the peril that awaits along the path. The creative process is all about exploration and experimentation, which can be utterly terrifying for those who have never dabbled in these particular areas. Take comfort in knowing that it doesn't go smoothly for anyone.

Press forward, and then press forward again. Dismiss criticism and consider constructive critique, even that which comes from your own mind.

For those who intend to distribute your book, keep in mind the benefits and things to be wary of when it comes to editing. Don't just worry about editors and beta readers; think about yourself and your relentless desire to pick things to bits *ad nauseam*. Learn when to make peace with, not pieces of your book. Find a way to let go and let it fly.

So how do you feel now? Ready to write a book? Take it one step at a time. When you get overwhelmed, pause yourself. Always maintain forward momentum. Don't get inside your own head.

Above all: Revel in every moment of the creative process. Even the not-so-lovely ones.

Good luck. May your fingers be swift and your muse always close at hand!

Resources

The following resources are intended to help inspire and excite you as a new writer. All sources have been credited where possible. Please don't consider the inclusion of any of these links as endorsements or partnerships; we aren't getting paid for sharing them, either. Consider this your friendly author friend sharing with you some interesting things that help them with this process.

The following sections outline all of the things you were promised in the main text, and then some. I've included a variety of resources that will help you get out of sticky situations and guide you through some organizational strategies, all to keep that forward momentum and productivity rolling.

Enjoy at your own leisure, and remember, truly nothing in this world is beloved by all... not even cheese. I've made it a point to include a few different varieties of each resource, but if none of these suit your particular methods, use this as a launchpad for discovering your own way!

Writing Exercises

Writing truly is an exercise for the mind, spirit, and body. From time to time, you may find yourself lacking in whatever mojo gets the creative juices flowing. When that happens, consider a writing exercise or two to help you navigate back to a space where imagination is more possible and thoughts are more organized. I've included many different types of writing exercises, neither of which is exclusively intended for writers of fiction or nonfiction. Basically, any time you find yourself falling off track, feel free to employ one of these exercises to help you find the way back to the path.

Eventually, you'll feel your flow return. If not, choose a different writing exercise, move on to brain cleansers, or grab a cup of tea and come back to it.

This is not a comprehensive list of exercises. These are just a few examples that I use in my own work. Feel free to look up even more exercises to help your imagination soar.

> 1. "Narrate Your Day." This one is fun because you don't even have to write anything down. This exercise is best in situations where you just can't get the words to appear, and you feel like you can't remember how to write.

To narrate your day, explain to yourself what you're doing at the moment. If you're a bit low on verbs at the moment, you can describe your surroundings. Don't think too much about it, just start describing:

"I sit perpendicular to a window. On my desk, which was once tragically painted white, a monitor glows bright white in the quickly dimming room."

"I was brushing my teeth. There was not enough toothpaste on the brush, but I lacked the concern to do anything about it. With my luck, I'd drop the toothbrush in the toilet if I tried to change anything about the situation. Best to let it ride."

Start with something obvious and real. Expand upon it. Add description. Give it life. Repeat.

    1. "This Is My..." *This* is another description exercise. I like to use this one when I'm trying to set a scene, bring a character to life, or really drive home a particular piece of evidence, but I seem to have forgotten all of my words.

For this exercise, choose an object. Any object, as long as you can actually see it and experience it in person at this exact moment. Start with the words "This is my," followed by the name of the object. Then describe it. Don't worry about it making sense right away. Just start writing out your description, then keep going until you run out of things to say about it. Then keep going. Eventually, you will run out of things to say about your trinket or geejaw, but keep pushing yourself to say more, whether that means adding more adjectives and adverbs, or including its significance in this universe.

    1. "I Read the News Today, Oh Boy." I like this one when I'm having trouble making connections happen or when I need to get over my own ego. You'll need some form of physical media that includes pictures and words, such as a newspaper, magazine, brochure, or catalog.

Find a picture of a person. That's your protagonist. Find another picture of a person. That's your antagonist. Find a sentence that includes an action verb, like "robbed a bank," or "receives a medal of honor." Write a little story in which those two people do the thing. Remember this is just garbage, and write off the head. Excuse typos. Ignore grammar. Freestyle it. Feign shock and surprise when it turns out pretty good and definitely worth putting a little more effort into developing. Finish one book before you start another.

    1. "Get Out." This is a bit of more traditional journaling, with

a tad bit of therapy attached. Basically, you'll free-write your way to mental freedom. Prepare a blank page. Close your eyes. Write. Every thought, make it come out. Think of it as clearing your cache.

Prompts

Many people use the terms "writing exercises" and "writing prompts" interchangeably. This isn't incorrect, but for the purpose of this book, I'm using "prompts" to describe mechanisms for getting unstuck when you've found yourself in a rut.

Use these prompts to help you redirect and refocus when you feel like you're repeating yourself, not saying enough, or "sounding dumb." Reach out and grab onto these prompts like a carrot on a stick- they can help pull you to safety!

1. Select a specific person in your life, and tell them what comes next. You can actually do this, or perform this exercise mentally. For example, "Ok, Meemaw, so after our hero goes to the castle, there's going to be a dragon, right? And the dragon is not going to see our hero, because... because... because he's under a sleeping spell!"

2. Stop acting like you're writing, and act like you're talking to someone. I strongly recommend you make a note to yourself in your writing journal about the exact page you were on when you implemented this prompt because things might get a little weird. Write exactly like you would speak, even if that includes curse words or colloquialisms, song lyrics, or whatever. You will inevitably find yourself naturally "talking" your way back into the book's original format.

3. Look up synonyms. This may sound strange, but looking at words can sometimes reignite a mind that's been simmering on low for too long. I once submitted an article for publication thinking I'd done a good job. The editor asked me if I had realized I used the word "influence" ten times in a single paragraph, and that two paragraphs covered the same information in different manners. My brain had clearly been stagnant. Looking up other words helped me diversify my thinking process and move forward meaningfully.

4. Ask yourself "Why". Children are very good at asking why things are the way they are, but adults tend to lose this sense of wonder. When you find yourself stumbling around, trying in vain to describe something or some piece of data, stop wandering and ask "Why?"

- Why did this happen?

- Why do I need to know this?

- Why am I explaining this now?

- Why does the reader care?

Character Map Examples

For my fiction-writing friends, here are a few samples and templates to help you organize your characters. As discussed earlier, the purpose of a character map is to keep you from forgetting who is who and who does what. Additionally, a character map can help you discover more and more interesting traits regarding your characters. Each of these examples is quite different, so take a look, give each a try, and decide what you need to keep the citizens of your new world in line.

This particular form allows you to truly discover who your characters are as human beings. This is possibly the most detailed version I've found yet: http://www.epiguide.com/ep101/writing/charchart.html

Some of the ins and outs of character mapping techniques, along with great examples:

https://www.thenovelry.com/blog/character-map

Here's a technique that involves a family-tree style map, as well as tips on organizing their biographies:

http://writeonsisters.com/writing-craft/6-easy-steps-to-great-character-mapping/This link leads to an online shop for teachers to share and sell character map templates. The prices are quite reasonable, especially for a resource you'll enjoy many times over!

https://www.teacherspayteachers.com/Browse/Search:character%20map%20template

Plot Outline Examples

If you do a simple search for "plot outlines" or "plot diagrams," you'll more than likely find a drawing of a line that rises slowly, reaches a peak, and then plummets swiftly. This drawing is the simplest explanation for a plot. As a writer, you'll find that your plot more greatly resembles a distressed spider's web than a beautiful single line; however, I cannot argue that the simplest templates get the job done. Here are a few examples of plot outlines to help you get your own plot details situated.

This is obviously an example of someone's personal template, and I very much like the style and simplicity of it. If you're in the early stages of figuring out actions and reactions, give a sample like this a try.

https://karcherry.files.wordpress.com/2013/07/plot-outline1.jpg

This version is very handy for those who have multiple questions to answer throughout the course of your book. Very rarely is our hero focused on just one thing at a time. An outline like this will help you reveal and map the course of each source of strife.

https://diymfa.com/writing/mapping-out-your-story

This link leads to several different types of plot outline templates. I like #5 in particular, because that looks a lot like my own plot outlines. If you're not sure which version of a plot outline would best stimulate your brain, take a cruise through the examples here to try a few different options.

https://templatelab.com/story-outline/

And since we've used her works as an example several times, I thought it might be interesting to share with you how author J.K. Rowling put together the *Harry Potter* books. This article includes the handwritten plot outline for chapters 13–24 of *Harry Potter and the Order of the Phoenix*. Notice how she tracks all of the simultaneously existing storylines on the horizontal, then fills in the necessary developments to each story on the vertical, chapter by chapter.

http://blog.paperblanks.com/2013/05/j-k-rowling-book-outline/

Nonfiction Outline Examples

Nonfiction works also require significant prework, as we discovered in the second section of this book. The purpose of an outline is to help you figure out how to get from one important point in your discussion to another. You can use the outline to help you set the tone or to help you remember key resources or quotes to help drive your discourse forward.

In the interest of showing my own work, here's my own outline for this book. Basically, I started with the concept of "How to Write a Book." Then I quite literally went stream of consciousness for the outline so that I could nail down what I wanted to share. I'm sure you'll be able to spot the differences and similarities.

https://docs.google.com/document/d/1Pbv1obA4W_v_IlQYR MHP8VArTHyj-upb94CW1dq2474/edit?usp=sharing

As you can see, my method most reflects the standard outline method, also presented here.

https://writenonfictionnow.com/outlining-first-time-self-publish ed-authors/

One extra tidbit I'd like to add is that, if you are using quotes or specific sections of resources, it is very helpful to include a link for or the basic bibliographic information for that quote or resource in your outline so you don't struggle to find it later.

Here is the world-famous Scrivener outline method. This writer provides a video as well as an explanation as to how the method works for her, and some tips and tricks for using it.

https://authorbasics.com/using-scrivener-outline-non-fiction-bo ok/

There are a few different samples included in this link for different types of nonfiction. If you're writing a book that isn't a simple wander through points to be made and discussions to be had, this link will help you figure out a creative and enjoyable flow of thoughts for your audience.

https://laptrinhx.com/news/how-to-write-a-nonfiction-book-free -chapter-outlining-templates-oAZ8D5e/

Nonfiction Table Of Content Examples

My editors will be the first people to tell you that my inclusion of this topic is purely hypocritical since I really don't follow any particular format or template when I'm writing for myself. I abandoned the idea of following a format during my first year of copywriting when I discovered that every client has developed their own formatting, and it's best to forget what you were taught in school and do what the person with the money wants. However, as a new writer who has not been subjected to years of memorizing the nuances of various formats only to have them change before you can put them to use, you likely would like some help with formatting.

The following are sites that provide templates for creating a TOC for your nonfiction masterpiece.

This link includes a variety of formats and templates, ranging from the highly stylistic to the very structured. Remember that you are using the TOC to help you organize and stay on track, and choose a version that is right for the task.

https://www.template.net/business/word-templates/table-of-con tents/

I like this guide from Sam Houston University (again, I have no affiliation with them; I simply like this link) because it demonstrates the full scholarly version of the table of contents, which you will note I personally have completely disregarded. If you are going to be shopping your work to a publisher, you'll most likely need to write this more formal APA version of a TOC in your final draft before shipping it off...

https://shsulibraryguides.org/thesisguide/tableofcontents

...unless you're using the Chicago style, in which case, you'll want to click on this link, instead.

https://www.scientific-editing.info/blog/chicago-table-of-content s/

Types of Nonfiction Organization / Formats

If you just saw the words "APA" and "Chicago" in the section above and had a mild wave of anxiety pass over you because you don't know what those are, here they are. As mentioned in the chapter regarding the organization or format of your piece, there are quite a few different methods, none of which are super important unless you're looking to publish your piece or place it under formal review. Again, I'm a very naughty writer who has used a mish-mash of styles for this book, but it's pretty clear by now that this is a very casual, candid piece, and not a scholarly work.

Check out the following links, and decide which feels more natural for you. If you are submitting your work for publishing or review, double-check with the publisher regarding their exact formatting requirements.

APA: American Psychological Association. Yes, really. Their preferred publishing format has been adopted across the writing community for scholarly pieces.

https://apastyle.apa.org/

Chicago: Developed in 1906 by the University of Chicago Press, this style is usually associated with topics surrounding business, arts, history, and humanities.

https://www.chicagomanualofstyle.org/home.html

MLA: The Modern Language Association developed this format in 1833, and it's changed several times since then. Currently, in their 9th edition, MLA sells handbooks, though some rules and tips are provided free of charge online. This style is generally applied to studies of language, culture, and human interest, and is very popular with college professors.

https://style.mla.org/mla-format

MECE: This is not a publication format, but rather an organizational formatting option. It's somewhat controversial; however, for those who tend to go off on stream-of-consciousness tangents when writing, it can help provide a little discipline when organizing your nonfiction piece.

https://www.caseinterview.com/mece

Desk Exercises

Writing is hard on the body as well as the mind, especially if you're not used to sitting down and wiggling your fingers to make words appear for hours at a time. You may find your back, posterior, legs, hips, arms, and fingers aching after your first few sessions.

Additionally, a stagnant body can lead to a bored mind, which is not helpful when you're trying to be creative. Get up and move every 30 minutes or so, or when you find yourself at a loss for words.

In reading these links, please note that I am not a doctor, and nothing I write should be considered medical advice. Always address discomfort with a trained physician.

This link offers loads of exercises you can do without leaving your desk, though you should definitely leave your desk every once in a while!

https://www.healthline.com/health/fitness/office-exercises

You're going to have to get up from your desk to do these exercises, but you'll be glad you did:

https://yogawithadriene.com/yoga-for-writers/

Here are some hand and wrist exercises to help you keep limber in between sessions:

https://www.webmd.com/osteoarthritis/ss/slideshow-hand-finger-exercises

This link provides some excellent options for getting your cardio in while psychologically chained to your writing. Plus, it uses the term "Deskercise," which I adore.

https://greatist.com/fitness/deskercise-33-ways-exercise-work

Brain Cleansers

Brain cleansers are exercises for your mind and emotions. Writing can be draining, especially if you're very passionate about what you're writing or simply feeling stressed by any part of the process. Stress is normal and can be good, but too much leads to writer's block, headaches, or worse-- quitting.

If you feel yourself getting overwhelmed, here are a few things you can do to chill out and get back on task.

Yoga Nidra:

Yoga Nidra is an excellent relaxation and centering technique that allows you to bring awareness to each part of your body individually. A form of meditation that can reorganize a frazzled brain, it can also bring your brain into a state of restfulness without that post-nap grogginess.

I don't know this person or have any affiliation with their YouTube channel, but I do appreciate the variety of practices offered here.

https://www.youtube.com/c/SarovaraYoga

For those who would like to learn more about the practice, a colleague of mine has written a book on the topic that gives a great introduction. This person I do know, but I'm not getting any kickbacks for mentioning her book:

https://www.amazon.com/Nidra-Yoga-beginners-increase-productivity-ebook/dp/B07ZQR81PT/ref=tmm_kin_swatch_0?_encoding=UTF8&qid=1635527242&sr=8-1

Games:

Depending on where your stress levels have taken you, you might prefer playing a game to help you return to your regular functional self. These games have been recommended for those looking to tune back into themselves and leave the chaos behind.

https://www.self.com/story/free-mobile-games

These, on the other hand, will spark greater activity in the brain.

https://www.lifehack.org/articles/technology/11-brain-training-apps-train-your-mind-and-improve-memory.html

Breathing Exercises:

You may not connect breathing with your brain, but when the thoughts stop and your heart starts racing, focusing on your breath can restore harmony in your body.

https://www.uofmhealth.org/health-library/uz2255

https://www.youtube.com/watch?v=MlaSf1D9tbA

https://yogawithadriene.com/free-yoga-videos/pranayama/

How to Get Published

Since I glossed over this topic earlier, I've included a few helpful resources to help guide you further along with the various publication options mentioned earlier.

Ghostwriting:

The steps and tricks you'll need to keep in mind when getting started as a ghostwriter

https://thewritelife.com/how-to-become-a-ghostwriter/

Some things to consider before you take the plunge

https://theregalwriter.com/2020/10/09/know-the-pros-and-cons-of-ghostwriting/

Self-publishing:

Where you can go to get your book self-published

https://selfpublishing.com/self-publishing-companies/

Amazon's guide to self-publishing

https://kdp.amazon.com/en_US/

How to get started with the process, and know whether it's ideal for you

https://knliterary.com/how-to-self-publish-a-book/

Traditional publishing:

This guide provides very detailed and solid information on both self and traditional publishing

https://writersdigestshop.com/pages/how-to-publish-a-book-an-overview-of-traditional-self-publishing

This guide includes real authors talking about the process and the various considerations of traditional publishing

https://getpublished.penguin.co.uk/

This article includes links to some common resources for finding and wooing a literary agent https://shutupwrite.com/how-to-find-a-literary-agent/

Communities for New Writers

For those looking for support, encouragement, critique, or validation, here are some links to online forums or communities dedicated to new writers. I cannot speak for the overall quality or politeness of all communities, so I encourage you to read and lurk a bit before you start joining in the discussion. Like all groups of people, some will be ideal for you, and others will not. Proceed at your own risk.

Writing Forums: https://www.writingforums.com/

She Writes: https://www.shewrites.com/

NaNoWriMo: https://nanowrimo.org/

Critique Circle: https://new.critiquecircle.com/landing

Go forth, be bold, and write a book!

About the Author

Lauren Bingham grew up in a house full of books. A dedicated bib-liophile by first grade, she often got into trouble for voraciously con-suming any written material—from consuming Reader's Digest cover to cover in one sitting to completing library books before they even made it home.

Lauren has been avidly writing for pure passion since childhood, and thanks to the internet for providing a comfortable place where all writers are welcome. Ghostwriting and copywriting since the early 2000s, she believes strongly that there is a story in each of us, and that any time is a great time to share those stories with others.

If you're interested in learning to write books, chances are high that you've tried before and gotten stuck. As a result, you may be even less enthusiastic about trying again. If that's the case, check out some personally selected writing exercises from author Lauren Bingham's vault of helpful tricks and tips for getting the cursor moving again... or for the first time.

Also by Lauren Bingham

One Word at a Time: How to Write a Fiction Book for Beginners
https://www.amazon.com/dp/B09ZFH296N

Non-Fiction for Newbies: How to Write a Factual Book and Actually
Kind of Enjoy It
https://www.amazon.com/dp/B0CCZWGB3N

R eviews and feedback help improve this book and the author.
If you enjoy this book, we would greatly appreciate it if you
could take a few moments to share your opinion and post a review on
Amazon. Thank you!

5 Writing Exercises

If you're interested in learning to write books, chances are high that you've tried before and gotten stuck. As a result, you may be even less enthusiastic about trying again. If that's the case, check out some personally selected writing exercises from author Lauren Bingham's vault of helpful tricks and tips for getting the cursor moving again... or for the first time. Go to https://subscribepage.io/5-Writing-Exe rciseto download your own copy of Lauren Bingham's Five Favorite Writing Exercises.

Made in United States
Orlando, FL
14 December 2024

55455640R00065